Overcoming

Fear, Worry, and Anxiety

Elyse Fitzpatrick

D0181604

HARVEST HOUSE PUBLISHERS
Eugene, OR 97402

Cover by Koechel Peterson & Associates, Minneapolis, Minnesota

OVERCOMING FEAR, WORRY, AND ANXIETY
Copyright © 2001 by Elyse Fitzpatrick
Published by Harvest House Publishers
Eugene, Oregon 97402
www.harvesthousepublishers.com

Library of Congress Cataloging-in-Publication Data
Fitzpatrick, Elyse, 1950–
 Overcoming fear, worry, and anxiety / Elyse Fitzpatrick.
  p. cm.
 ISBN-13: 978-0-7369-0589-3
 ISBN-10: 0-7369-0589-8
 1. Christian women—Religious life. 2. Fear—Religious aspects—Christianity.
 I. Title.

BV4527.F59 2001
248'43—dc21   2001024088

Printed in the United States of America

07 08 09 10 11 12 13 14 / BC-MS / 14 13 12 11 10 9 8 7

Contents

Acknowledgments

Every sentence in this book is a mere reflection of God's mercy to me in surrounding me with godly people who know the truth and how it applies to life. Among these people are Jay E. Adams, George Scipione of The Institute for Biblical Counseling and Discipleship, the staff of The National Association of Nouthetic Counselors, The Biblical Counseling Foundation, and The Christian Counseling and Educational Foundation. Wherever this book is correct, it is simply a fusion of what I've learned from them.

God also sent comfort to me in the form of friends who have consistently prayed for and encouraged me. Foremost among these friends are Anita Manata, Donna Turner, Julie Pascoe, Hannah and Barbara Duguid, Jason and Kristin Barrie, Betsy Smith, Bonnie Graham, and Eileen Scipione from IBCD, and the dear people at North City Presbyterian Church. As always, the staff of Evangelical Bible Book Store, particularly John Hickernell, has been of invaluable assistance. My editor, Steve Miller from Harvest House, is a valued friend and has been a constant source of encouragement.

The ones who have sacrificed most have been my family and particularly my patient and loving husband, Phil. *Thank you, dear.* James, Cody and Jessica, Joel and Ruth, and Wesley and Hayden have waited patiently while I spent hours locked in my office. *Dear ones: If anyone is helped through this book, you can know that you had a part in it.* And, of course, thanks again, Mom, for all your inspiration and helpful editing.

James, Joel, Cody, Wesley, and Hayden
May my sons and their sons be filled with the fear of the Lord
and stand strong in the truth that will enable them
to acquit themselves like men.

A Genuinely *Mad* Hatter: Paralyzed by Fear

The auditorium was filled with the proud parents of the most promising advanced drama students in the county. Backstage, members of each cast were hastily reviewing their lines, getting ready for their turn to compete.

"You're on next," said our teacher, Mrs. Archer. "Just remember what we've worked on and…break a leg." We all smiled at each other, knowing that the phrase "break a leg" was thespian-speak for "good luck." We didn't think we needed luck; we had gone over our lines so many times that they seemed second nature to us. We felt confident—and why shouldn't we? After all we were the best. As the five of us, actors and actresses who were dramatizing Alice's famous tea party, walked on stage, the crowd fell silent and the lights went up.

"I just love a tea party," Alice said to me, the Mad Hatter. As she sat there looking at me, waiting for me to respond with my lines, something utterly shocking happened. I suddenly felt like I was watching the whole scene as a bystander—everything became fuzzy and it seemed as though I was losing touch with reality. In the back of my mind, I knew I should be doing something. *Wasn't there something I should say?* As seconds that felt like hours ticked by, I became more and more disoriented. My hands were sweating and my heart was pounding. I felt like I was going to faint. Somewhere in the back of my mind I vaguely heard our teacher frantically whispering my lines to me from offstage. *Was I supposed to say those lines?* I couldn't even remember how to speak. Nothing that was happening around me made any sense.

"I just love a tea party," Alice said again, this time glaring at me. I wanted to respond, to make her happy, but deep inside my heart I couldn't figure out what she wanted. I didn't know who I was or what I was doing out there with all those lights on me. The audience began to murmur. My fellow actors and actresses stared unbelievingly at me. I just sat there, at the end of the table, in a daze. *Who was I...what was happening to me?* All I could think of was how to escape. So I just stood up and wandered offstage. The rest of the cast, humiliated and angry, soon followed.

You know, I can vividly recall that scene even though it occurred more than 30 years ago. It's frozen in my mind along with all the other grand humiliations of my life. I'd like to tell you that I went backstage, snapped out of it, and went on with our presentation, but that wouldn't be the truth. No, in fact, that was the end of my big chance at "stardom," as well as some friendships in my drama class. That day I felt more like a *Mad Hatter* than I had ever wanted to.

Fear is incredibly powerful, isn't it? It can wipe out your memory and cause your heart to pound. In fact, it can paralyze you. It can cause a trained soldier to melt into a sobbing child just like the terrified infantryman in the movie *Saving Private Ryan*. He knew that he should get up and save his buddy but he felt completely unable to move.

As we spend time together looking at our fears and anxieties, I'm going to share more of these moments with you—both from my own life and the lives of others. From the grand humiliations to the nagging little anxieties that dance like specters around the edges of our thoughts, I want you to know that you're not alone. I know what it is to lay awake at night with that feeling of foreboding, thinking, *Things are too good, this can't last,* or *Things are so awful, this will never change!* I know what it is to worry, to feel the muscles tightening in my neck, and to feel my stomach churning. I've spent days wrestling with the thought that *everything* is on the verge of collapse. I've let my mind run down every little rabbit trail—imagining that the children are dead or my husband has lost his love for me or that I have some dread disease or...and on and on it goes

In response to these fear-filled thoughts, I've said and done some very foolish things. Some of them, in hindsight, are actually quite humorous, while others have left a trail of sad consequences. I'm purposely going to share many of these personal incidents with you so that you'll come to see that we're all alike in our emotional responses. I'll also share some stories of women I've counseled—women just like you and me. I'm going to do this because I want you to know that *you're not alone.*

In fact, that's exactly what the Bible teaches: "No temptation has overtaken you but such as is common to man..." (1 Corinthians 10:13). The fears you and I face really aren't all that unique; this verse teaches that we're all pretty much in the same boat. Although the focus and intensity of our fears may be different, every person who has ever lived has had to struggle against them. Perhaps from your perspective it doesn't seem that way, but even those who appear to be the most brave among us have had to overcome fear.

The One Who Conquered Fear

This isn't only a book about our common struggles and failures. Even though it's helpful for us to know that we're not alone, I realize the awareness of that fact won't help us to overcome the problem. The passengers on the *Titanic* might have been glad to have someone's hand to hold, but in the end that didn't stop the ship from sinking beneath that frigid water. No, just like them, we need someone strong enough to rescue us from the blackness of night and the terrifying cold that threatens to benumb our souls. We need someone who is stronger than our fears.

Jesus Christ is that someone. He's the only one who intimately knows all our thoughts and fears. He's the only one who is able to deliver us. That's because He's faced the greatest of all fears for us—the fear of death and separation from God—and He's come through victorious. The Bible teaches that one reason He left heaven and came to earth was to "deliver those who through fear...have been living all their lives as slaves to constant dread" (Hebrews 2:15 TLB).

Our fears are like chains around our hearts—they paralyze, entrap, and enslave us. But Jesus Christ holds the key that can unlock and banish all your fears. He's able to do this because His love is more powerful than your fears. It's His plan to teach, encourage, and transform you into a person who trusts Him—even in the face of your deepest worries and anxieties. He doesn't promise to make you perfect here on earth, but He does promise to work mightily in your heart now and will ultimately, in heaven, completely free you from every fear.

Jesus' promise is available to every Christian. Don't assume this book is written only for people who have a deep knowledge of the Bible. What's key is that you are a child of God, one who has received Jesus Christ as your personal Savior and Lord.

If you aren't sure whether you're a Christian or not, stop right now and turn to Appendix A in the back of this book. It's there that you'll discover God's plan to remake you into a new person. Just think—perhaps God will use your struggle with your fears to bring you to Himself. Don't be afraid that God will reject you if you don't understand everything about the Christian life. If you know that you need a Savior, then He's calling to you today.

The Journey to Freedom

Since the day that I wandered off the stage in a daze so many years ago, God has transformed my life. I've spoken in front of large crowds and done many radio and television interviews.

I recognize that this change is a result of God's powerful work in my life. I'm not asking you to put your trust in me or my words. I can see how I've grown because of God's kindness in my life, but in many ways I'm still so weak. What I've written here is not offered as the answer to all your problems, but it will point you to one who is.

So why not begin your journey through this book by asking God to help you put your trust in Him? After all, He's the only one who has ever conquered fear and death, and He's the only one who can transform you. He's the Heart-Changer and He's more interested in freeing you than you could possibly know. So, bow your heart before Him, roll up your sleeves, and let's begin our journey toward freedom.

CHAPTER

I

Understanding
How Fear Works

*"Such strange creatures are we that we probably
smart more under blows which never fall upon us
than we do under those which do actually come."*[1]

—CHARLES H. SPURGEON
Nineteenth-century British author and preacher

I had known Kathryn for a number of years before she
came to talk to me. Kathryn seemed to be a dependable, hard-
working woman who had a strong faith. Even though she was
shy, she obviously made real efforts to maintain friendships in
our church and in the community.

As our time together began, I became aware of problems in
her life that I had never before suspected. Kathryn said that she
was becoming increasingly fearful and that she was worried
that she might be developing agoraphobia. *Agoraphobia* is the
name commonly given to a way of responding to life that leads
to the avoidance of certain activities or situations. An agora-
phobic might seek to avoid things like driving, standing in
line, shopping, or attending meetings or social gatherings, and
might even refuse to leave the house.

As Kathryn continued to share her story with me, I saw how
painful it was for her to admit that she was afraid to go shopping at our local indoor mall. The reason for her fear? She was
afraid that being trapped too far from an exit door would cause

her to become nauseated and throw up. Kathryn's fear had become a noose around her neck that tightened daily and kept her tethered more and more closely to home. Kathryn was experiencing the truth of Spurgeon's words: "our groundless fears are our chief tormentors."[2]

Kathryn knew that her fear was unreasonable, especially because what she feared—vomiting at the mall—had never actually happened to her. Her confusion was compounded by the guilt she felt because she was causing problems for the family and particularly her husband. She also believed that her unreasonable fears were sinful, so she was anxious about her salvation and thought she was a disappointment to the Lord.

What was going on in Kathryn's life? Did she have some bizarre mystical problem? Did she just need to pray or read her Bible more? Could she even find, in the Bible, concrete answers for her problem? Just what was this emotion that seemed to rule her, and where did these feelings come from?

Understanding the Physical Side of Fear

In upcoming chapters we're going take an in-depth look at fear, its causes, and consequences. We're going to consider what the Bible says about why we become fearful and how to grow past our fears. But first, let's begin by taking a look at the physical side of this emotion.[3] Like all of our emotions, fear is experienced both in our mind and in our body, causing intense physical responses.

Physically, *fear is a felt reaction to perceived danger*. Because God loved us, He created us with the ability to respond quickly to danger. Here's an example: Imagine that you've just noticed that your car has stopped on a railroad track. You hear a whistle and look up to see that a train is headed right for you. As soon as these facts register in your brain, your body automatically goes into "overdrive." Your brain receives the warning that danger is imminent and orders your body to quickly release a number of hormones, including adrenaline. Once these hormones are released into the bloodstream, certain physical changes will immediately take place. Your muscles will tense up to prepare you for action. Your heart rate and breathing will quicken to supply you with extra oxygen and strength. Even your eyesight and hearing will become more acute. Your foot will then punch the accelerator pedal to the floor and you'll move more quickly than you ever thought possible. All of these changes will occur instantaneously, in a moment's time.

Whenever we find ourselves confronted with danger, it's easy to see how God's grace reaches even to the way that we've been created. The physical attributes that help to protect us from danger are truly a good gift, aren't they? God's design of our body is amazing, as Psalm 139 says: "I am fearfully and wonderfully made" (verse 14). God has gifted us with these physical abilities so that we can survive in what is sometimes a dangerous world.

You'll notice that I said that fear is a felt reaction to a *perceived* danger. I purposely defined fear in that way because sometimes our minds perceive or imagine a danger that isn't really there. Everyone has experienced the sensation of awakening from a nightmare with a pounding heart and quickened breath. At these times, the danger that our body is reacting to is entirely in our mind. In spite of this, our body responds as though we faced a real threat. As you can see, our minds do affect our bodies in very powerful ways—and Kathryn recognized this.

Kathryn's fear that she might throw up in the mall was irrational. Even though her fear was groundless, her body wasn't able to differentiate between true and false alarms. It simply responded the way that it was supposed to. It didn't matter that the danger wasn't legitimate. Whenever she went to the mall she was afraid that she would experience all the physical changes that she dreaded, and her fear caused her to feel nauseous and convinced her that she probably was going to lose control and embarrass herself. You see, she'd actually become afraid that she was going to be fearful.

Not only do our bodies respond to fear by equipping us to *avoid* or *attack* danger; there are also times when our bodily chemicals influence us in more subtle ways. If we are busy attending to other business or if we become used to running at high levels of stress, sometimes we won't notice the changes taking place. We won't know what's happening in our bodies until some incident occurs that makes it evident.

Oops! Pardon Me, My Anxieties Are Showing

My husband, Phil, and I live in San Diego, California, a city on the U.S./Mexican border. We've made many trips into Mexico, and I always dread the passage over the border from Mexico back into the United States. At this most-traversed border crossing in the world, the lines are almost always long and the wait to get up to the checkpoint is both tedious and nerve-wracking.

On one particular occasion when my husband and I were crossing back over into the States we both received quite a surprise. Part of the routine practiced by the Border Patrol officers is to ask travelers two questions: What is your citizenship? and What are you bringing back from Mexico? Phil and I both replied, "United States" to the first question, and then I responded, "Fruit" to the second. You can't imagine our shock at my response! The reason was because we *hadn't* brought any fruit from Mexico, and we knew that bringing fruit across the border was illegal. We both just sat there, aghast and amazed, with our mouths hanging open. Finally I regained my composure and said, "I mean nothing." Fortunately, the officer merely looked at me like I was crazy and waved us through. All the way home Phil kept looking at me with sideways glances—I think he thought he knew where the real fruit was!

In this mildly humorous incident, I didn't know how fearful and stressed I was about crossing the border until my actions made me aware of it. It was this incident that opened my eyes to my unnecessary nervousness at the border and also to my blindness toward my true emotional state.

The Vicious Cycle

Fear not only affects your body and your behavior, but the reverse is true as well. If you're a person with a predisposition to react fearfully, you'll be more likely to experience the physical symptoms of fear if you drink too much caffeine, eat too much sugar, or don't get sufficient rest or exercise.[4]

If you generally feel stressed about your responsibilities or fearful about your life, you won't feel comfortable relaxing and you probably won't take the time to eat properly or exercise. The inability to relax or sleep soundly will heighten your sensitivity to alarm and danger, causing more adrenaline to be released into your body, which, in turn, can bring on even more sleep problems. Drinking caffeine to overcome the tired and sluggish feeling caused by lack of sleep will then simply compound the problem.

From this brief overview, you can see how easily fear can begin a vicious cycle of runaway thoughts, physical responses, imaginations, and neglected care of the body that can serve to bring about more fear and heightened physical responses. It's easy to see how the results of fear may create more fear, leading toward total slavery.

Fear Is Habitual

Judith, a woman who struggled with habitual fear, worked as a certified nurse assistant in a local convalescent home. Like Kathryn, she had a strong faith in God and wanted to please Him. She came in to talk with me because she was having problems at her work. She found that every time she walked into the room of a seriously ill patient, she would feel overwhelmed by terror. Her body would react with symptoms such as a pounding heart, chest pain, shortness of breath, and weakness. She was terrified that she was going to faint or that she might frighten her patient or harm him in some way. She felt out of control and thought she might be going crazy. I could tell that she really enjoyed her job but was afraid that she might have to change careers. In fact, her problems with some patients had gotten so serious that they had created resentments with the other nurse assistants and conflicts with her supervisor.

As we discussed her difficulties, she said that she had tried to overcome her fears by praying every morning and asking God to help her to not think about her fear. She wasn't aware of any fearful thoughts that triggered her feelings of panic; it seemed as though they just came out of nowhere.

Fear, like everything else in life, can become habitual. In fact, it can become such an ingrained habit that it really does seem like it comes out of nowhere. People who have experienced what are commonly called *panic attacks* report sudden occurrences of intense anxiety that don't seem to have any basis in their thoughts. This intense experience can seem so mysterious and baffling that the fear of it can easily become a controlling factor in a sufferer's life.

Let me illustrate how emotional responses can become habitual.[5] Think about the process of walking down a set of stairs. When you use the stairs for the first time, you're conscious of each step and you carefully look where you're going so that you don't fall. But if the stairs become a part of your daily routine, you'll quickly develop a habit of going down them without a thought. You might even be able to carry on a conversation or call someone on your cell phone while traversing the steps that you once had to concentrate on. Eventually you won't even be conscious of them at all. In fact, if you're an athletic sort, you might even take them two or three at a time. Or you might even sit on the banister and slide down just for fun.

Now, if on your first attempt down the stairs you had *imagined* what it would be like to jump from the top all the way to the bottom in one leap, then you would probably become afraid and develop feelings of nervousness as you actually walk down. If your fear persists, it could become habitual. Even though in your mind you know that your fear is unreasonable, still, it will have an effect on you because of how you've allowed your perception to be influenced by your imagination.

Now, a panic attack is like jumping from the top stair to the bottom in our thinking process. Rather than taking a situation step by step (as we should when walking a staircase), we jump quickly from our initial thought to full-blown panic.

For instance, Judith was surprised when she remembered that the first time she experienced a feeling of panic was when trying to care for her overly demanding chronically ill father. She loved him and was afraid that she might displease him or harm him by bringing the wrong medication. As a young child, she responded to caregiving situations with fear. As she thought back on her childhood, she realized that she had gone into nursing because she enjoyed helping others, but she still harbored anxieties about making a mistake or being disapproved of by others. She wasn't aware of her fears during her teen or college years, but when she returned to taking care of seriously ill persons, she responded just as she had as a child. You can see how Judith's fear, although irrational in her situation, had its basis in rational thought and experience.

As we talked, Judith remembered another situation that seemed pertinent. When she first went to work at the convalescent home where she was employed, one of her patients suddenly went into cardiac arrest. Judith responded properly and notified her supervisor, but afterward she played the incident over and over in her mind. She was haunted by thoughts like, *What if the man had died? What if the supervisor couldn't help him? Was I responsible for his problem? How could I ever face a patient's family or myself if a patient dies?* These questions, and others like them, plagued her thoughts for a number of days until the incident faded from her memory. It wasn't until she began struggling with panic attacks at the bedsides of her patients that she became aware of the powerful effect this earlier experience had had on her.

People who suffer from panic attacks often report similar sensations. It seems that without any forethought or warning the body begins pumping adrenaline. That's what makes panic attacks and certain kinds of phobias, such as the fear of heights or closed-in spaces, so difficult to understand. Most sufferers aren't aware of any predisposing thoughts that bring about the sensation of fear. It just seems to come from nowhere. However, rather than being terribly mysterious, the truth about panic attacks and fears is really quite easy to understand. People experience them because they have developed a habit. When they're in any given situation, they don't even need to think about their fears—they just react. The mind works so quickly and habitually that mentally they jump from the top step to the bottom step without any effort. This, in turn, makes them think that their emotions are out of control or that they're going crazy. They then begin to try to avoid these "out of control" situations, which allows the habit to become more and more paralyzing.

Some people struggle with fears in social situations. They fear that they will say or do something that will appear foolish and so they avoid them. Others have fears about illness or dying, while still others fear having to speak to strangers or in front of large audiences. Some people avoid intimate relationships, even though they are lonely and desire to be married, simply because they are fearful that they might make a mistake or be let down. There are as many forms of fear as there are situations in life.

The Faces of Our Fears

As you can see, a person's predisposition to being fearful can be caused by a combination of things. First, it seems that some people, because of their basic personality, are more inclined in this direction than others. In the upcoming chapters, we'll take a much deeper look at the factors in our personality that make us fearful. Some people also seem to have sensitive bodies that react more acutely to fear, or they may be more aware of the changes taking place in their bodies.

Personal history also plays a significant role in one's ability to handle life's problems. If you grew up with fearful parents— a mother who was always retreating from life's difficulties, or a father who hid away—then it's more likely you will be fearful. If you grew up in a home where there was a high level of abuse or shame, or where you felt as though you could never please anyone, you'll probably struggle. But your childhood history isn't the only significant history that you have. You also have your adult experiences, which in many cases are more significant than what happened to you when you were younger. For instance, if you've had a hard time getting a job, the more you interview unsuccessfully, the more fearful you'll become of meeting people and trying to sell your skills, and hence, the more trouble you'll have finding work.

Finally, we're all a product of how we've responded to the specific life God has marked out for us. Some of our responses may have occurred in a spirit of faith, while others flowed out of unbelief. As we will note in upcoming chapters, our relationship with the Lord, particularly our understanding of who He is and the significance of His Word, will make all the difference in how we handle life's situations and our fears.

Our Common Heritage

The human experience of fear isn't anything new. Although it's probably discussed more now because we live in the information age, fear has been around almost since the beginning of time. As we progress through this book, we're going to take an in-depth look at the Bible's perspectives on fear, but for now, let's just take a quick peek at the first record of it in God's Word.

When God created the earth, the kind of fear that we've been talking about didn't exist. In the Garden of Eden, Adam and Eve were completely safe and free from harm. They didn't fear any predators or diseases. All of their physical needs were provided for. They loved their Creator, each other, and the work that He had given them to do. They probably didn't even know that such a thing as an end to life was possible. They didn't worry about what tomorrow would bring. They were completely safe, joyous, and filled with praise for their Lord.

Then the inconceivable happened: They sinned. First Eve and then Adam fell into Satan's trap and disobeyed God. The immediate result of their disobedience was fear and shame. Here's how the Bible describes the aftermath of that dreadful event:

> They [Adam and Eve] heard the sound of the Lord God walking in the garden in the cool of the day, and the man and his wife hid themselves from the presence of the Lord God among the trees of the garden. Then the Lord God called to the man, and said to him, "Where are you?" He said, "I heard the sound of You in the garden, and I was afraid because I was naked; so I hid myself."
> —Genesis 3:8-10

The initial response of Adam and Eve was fear, wasn't it? They were ashamed and afraid, so they hid themselves. They felt vulnerable and were uncomfortable about being seen as they were: naked. They no longer cherished the free and open fellowship they had known with God. They didn't want God to see them. They feared His displeasure, and rightly so. They had disobeyed Him, and their disobedience would forever set them up to hide, cover up, and cringe in slavish fear before Him. We whose lives are consistently characterized by fear cannot begin to imagine the immense tragedy of their loss; their relationship with their Creator and with one another would never be the same. Sin utterly devastated them...and this devastation continues today.

The Key to Freedom from Fear

As this book unfolds, you'll see how sin is a significant factor in our fearfulness. I can imagine that this might be a new or even uncomfortable concept for you. Perhaps you think that speaking about sin is condemning or unkind. It is true that sin, especially our own sin, is hard to look at. I know that is true for me.

However, I'm not going to direct your thoughts to your sin because I want to punish, condemn, or reject you. I'm going to direct you there because it's there, *and there alone,* that you'll discover the truth that will set you free. I trust that the Holy Spirit will gently convince you of your need to draw close to your Savior, and as He does that, you'll find the rest and help you long for.

My heartfelt desire is that this book will serve as a tool that draws you near to the one who loves you and who alone can forgive, transform, and restore you. So, don't be afraid to come out from behind that bush and look deeply into your own heart. It might be painful for a time, but by God's grace and mercy, it will be worth it. Look deeply also into the heart of the One who loved you so much that He walked into the jaws of death and His enemy's grasp for your sake. Love like that just demands to be trusted. So whether your fears are real or imagined—whether you're just beginning to understand them or you're too familiar with them—you can throw yourself on the mercy of God, the one who loves you more than you could possibly know.

For Further Thought

1. How would you describe the kinds of fears that you face?

2. How much of an influence is the "fear of fear" in your life?

3. How has your history (as a child and an adult) influenced your propensity to be fearful?

4. Can you think of any changes that you need to make in the way that you care for your body? What are some specific steps you can take?

5. Write out a prayer asking God to show you your need of Him and to grant you hope that you really can be free.

Bible Heroes
Who Struggled with Fear

"Fear is a more dangerous enemy
than those that you fear..."[1]

—THOMAS WATSON
Puritan author and pastor

*W*e Christians tend to talk a lot about the heroes of faith in the Bible. We look, sometimes superficially, at the people whose histories are written for us and we think, *They're so brave. Why can't I be like them?* Their lives seem so free from fear, they seem to stand strong in the face of difficult circumstances. *What's wrong with me?* we wonder. *If I'm a Christian, why do I struggle with anxiety? Why aren't I like these great heroes?*

It is true that God has worked powerfully in people's lives down through the ages. Hebrews chapter 11, which we'll look at more closely later, talks about the courageous faith of men like Moses and women like Sarah. However, if we look more carefully, we will notice that many of these heroes experienced major struggles with fear at some time. In fact, it was these struggles that made them stronger later in life. The Lord Jesus Christ is the only one who never succumbed to sinful fear, even though He was tempted to do so in the same ways that we are. So if we're going to look for heroes of faith, we'll have a pretty hard time finding more than one…but this one is enough.

Examples of Fear in the Bible

In this chapter, we're going to take some time to expand a little on the history of fear, or better yet, sinful fear, in the Bible. I think you'll be surprised and comforted to know that many of the heroes you are acquainted with in the Bible were people just like you: They struggled with fear. In this chapter we'll not only take a look at some of these individuals, but we'll also try to discern what motivated them to act the way they did. Let's begin at the book of beginnings, Genesis.

The Original Fear—Adam and Eve

As we learned earlier, fear was first introduced into human experience in the Garden. Adam and Eve had enjoyed sweet, confident fellowship with their Creator and with one another. Then they sinned. It was because of their sin—their broken relationship with one another and with God—that they first felt the consequences of fear: more fear, broken relationships, and shame. When they heard the Lord coming to visit them in the Garden, they hid themselves. Adam was afraid that God would see him as he was: exposed, vulnerable, and sinful. Adam's fear of God begat more and more ungodly imaginations of his Maker in his heart.

But even before Adam and Eve hid from God, fear was playing a part. What was it that caused Eve to disobey her Lord like that? We don't know. We can surmise that she feared she might be missing something that would be beneficial to her. She may have doubted God's wisdom and love. She might have been afraid that she needed something that God hadn't given her. It's hard to understand why she felt this way, but the Bible does say with certainty that she was deceived (2 Corinthians 11:3).

After pronouncing the judgment that Adam and Eve deserved, God mercifully covered them with animal skins.

Then He sent them out of the Garden. Never again would man know the kind of life he had known; never again would he be completely free from shame, embarrassment, self-consciousness, and fear.

But, thank God, that's not the end of the story. As Christians, God is restoring us to the same kind of fellowship and freedom that Adam and Eve knew, first with Himself and then with one another. Jesus' death is the means that God has used to break down the walls of separation between us (Romans 5:1). Although we'll never have what they had because we'll always struggle with our sin, we still can know significant joy and peace.

In Fear of Danger—Abraham

Earlier, I mentioned that even the great heroes of the Bible experienced fear and its consequences. A few chapters after Adam and Eve, we meet Abraham, a man often upheld as an example of one who had great faith. At certain times we see Abraham at his best: willingly and obediently leaving his country and traveling to an unknown land; sacrificially raising the knife that would take the life of his promised son, Isaac. Yes, there really are significant victories in Abraham's life, aren't there?

But then we see another side of him. Perhaps this is the side of Abraham that you'll more closely identify with. On two occasions during his travels, once to Egypt and once to a land called Gerar, Abraham lied to powerful men about Sarah, his beautiful wife. He told these men that she was his sister. Why? Because he thought that if the kings of these lands saw her and knew she was his wife, they would kill him so that they could take her for themselves. To put it bluntly, he wanted to save his own skin.

Abraham knew that Sarah was supposed to be the mother of God's chosen people, but he ignored God's plans and endangered her. It was only due to God's restraining grace that she didn't end up in a harem.[2] Because of his fear, he sinned against his wife, deceived rulers, was a source of trouble to them, and above all, dishonored God. Was Abraham's fear logical? Yes, probably so. Was it sinful? Yes, undoubtedly. Was God still able to use him and change him into a man of faith? Yes, and He can do the same with any of us.

Fear Caused by Doubt—Sarah

In 1 Peter, women are told to follow in the footsteps of Abraham's wife, Sarah. In some ways, she was a role model for godly women: She followed her husband, left her home, and set out for a land of promise—a land she had never seen.

But Sarah struggled with fears of her own. Her husband had told her of God's promise of a son, and as the years went by and she remained barren, she became more and more fearful. Her biological clock wasn't just ticking away; it had stopped. The Bible says that her womb "was dead." And so, in fear, she decided to take matters into her own hands. Abraham needed an heir, she longed for a son, and so she came up with a scheme. She gave her maid, Hagar, to her husband so that he might impregnate her and fulfill the promise. What a whirlwind of trouble her actions spawned! In fact, the trouble between the children of Israel and the children of Hagar, which began with the birth of Hagar's son Ishmael, has continued for centuries.

Later, the Lord came to visit Abraham. "In one year I will visit you and your wife will have a son," He said. Sarah, who was eavesdropping behind a tent curtain, laughed to herself. This wasn't the laughter of joy or mirth, it was the laughter of unbelief and cynicism. The Lord confronted her laughter of unbelief and said, "Is anything too difficult for the Lord?" But Sarah denied that she had laughed, saying, "I did not laugh." Why? Because she was afraid (Genesis 18:10-15).

Abraham and Sarah are held up in Scripture as examples of people of faith. Can you see how, in themselves, in their own power, they really weren't such great examples? What, then, makes them examples of faith? God's grace. *Grace* is God's unmerited favor on His children in spite of their faults. We're going to look deeply into the role that grace plays in overcoming fears in chapter 11, but for now I just want you to get a glimpse of how strong and loving God is. He worked in mighty ways through Abraham and Sarah in spite of their weaknesses, and He can do the same through you and me.

"I'm Not Good Enough"—Moses

The story of Moses is one that's pretty well known to most people. He was rescued from drowning by Pharaoh's daughter and brought up in Pharaoh's palace as her son. But, when God began to speak to him about delivering His people, Moses took affairs into his own hands and killed an Egyptian who was oppressing one of his fellow Israelites. Moses then had to flee into the wilderness for his life. Years went by, and in time Moses' dreams of being a deliverer faded. Then he had an encounter with a burning bush. As God outlined His plan for the release of His people, Moses became more and more afraid. Certainly the thought of returning to the most powerful nation on earth and demanding the freedom of slaves would be intimidating. As Moses considered God's call, his mind was filled with fears—primarily fears that he would be unsuccessful or that he wouldn't be able to complete the task. Consider what he said to God and see if his concerns resonate in your heart.

- "Moses said to God, 'Who am I, that I should go to Pharaoh, and that I should bring the sons of Israel out of Egypt?'" (Exodus 3:11)
- "Then Moses said, 'What if they will not believe me or listen to what I say? For they may say, 'The Lord has not appeared to you'" (Exodus 4:1).
- "Then Moses said to the Lord, 'Please, Lord, I have never been eloquent, neither recently nor in time past,

nor since You have spoken to Your servant; for I am slow of speech and slow of tongue'" (Exodus 4:10).

- "But he said, 'Please, Lord, now send the message by whomever You will'" (Exodus 4:13).

Trusting God, Not Self

I can really identify with Moses' fear, can't you? *I can't do that...I'm not good at public speaking...but what if they don't believe me.* Can't you just picture it? I can. In fact, I think I've had those kinds of conversations with the Lord. All along, God was encouraging Moses. He assured him of His presence and His power to accomplish His will. But all Moses could see was his own inadequacy, fear, and unbelief.

Notice that God didn't spend time trying to boost Moses' *self*-confidence. Rather, God kept reminding him that he should put his confidence in Him. Whenever we spend time trying to convince ourselves that we're really better or stronger or wiser than we know we are, we're doomed to failure. God doesn't want us to grow in self-confidence. He wants us to put all of our trust in Him. After all, He's the only one who's powerful enough to overcome the Pharaohs in our lives.

As Moses grew in his trust of the Lord, God used him to accomplish a great deliverance. In fact, Moses is now known as one of the greatest leaders in biblical history. But that wasn't because he was such a brave guy all on his own, was it? It was only because of God's great power and His determination to accomplish His purpose. And what God did for Moses, He can do for you. You can rest in the knowledge that if God is calling you to do something, even if it's just being brave enough to go to church and speak with people, then His grace will be effective in your life, too.

The Wrong Kind of Fear of God

The children of Israel had been slaves in Egypt for about 400 years when Moses led them out of bondage and on a wilderness journey that would take them to the Promised Land. Three months later, God told Moses to tell the people that He would meet with them. Moses told the people about the boundaries that the people had to respect because God's awesome presence was going to be near them. They gladly agreed to meet with God. But when they actually saw the manifestation of God so near, they became filled with terror.

> All the people perceived the thunder and the lightning flashes and the sound of the trumpet and the mountain smoking; and when the people saw it, they trembled and stood at a distance. Then they said to Moses, "Speak to us yourself and we will listen; but let not God speak to us, or we will die." Moses said to the people, "Do not be afraid...." So the people stood at a distance, while Moses approached the thick cloud where God was.
> —Exodus 20:18-21

It's interesting, isn't it, that Moses is the one telling the people not to be afraid? God's grace had worked powerfully in his heart, hadn't it? If you use your imagination, you won't have much trouble understanding why the Israelites responded in the way they did. Their senses were being overloaded by the thunder, lightning, loud trumpets, smoke, the ground quaking under their feet. If I had been one of them, I probably would have taken off in a hurry, too. The people were afraid of God and decided that it would be best to let Moses deal with Him alone. Then Moses could just report back to them. This God, Jehovah, was just a bit too scary and uncontrollable for them. As writer C. S. Lewis said about the lion Aslan, who represents Jesus Christ in Lewis's book series The Chronicles of Narnia, "He isn't a tame lion."[3] This servile fear that they felt towards God would breed more fear, sin, and hiding from Him. It would be the source of multiplied sorrows and failures.

In chapter 9 I'm going to talk about the right kind of fear of God—the kind of fear that draws us towards Him rather than pushing us away. What we'll call *godly fear* is commanded in the Bible in many places, as we'll see. Godly fear is also one of the key steps in overcoming what we'll call *sinful fear* from now on. Please remember that in calling our fear *sinful*, I'm not condemning you. Rather, I'm trying to help you clearly see God's plan to change and free you. This change starts with recognizing your need for a Savior…and none of us really does that until we see that we all are sinners in need of forgiveness and grace.

Helping you see the sinfulness of your fear may seem like a cruel thing to do. After all, you probably don't think you need something else to be afraid of! Should you now fear God's wrath or disapproval in addition to all your other fears? One of the goals of this book is to help you differentiate between fear that is good or godly, and fear that is bad or sinful. I want to encourage the good kind of fear in you—you'll learn that it's this kind of fear, coupled with love and grace, that will break the bonds that bind you so tightly today. So, please don't be afraid to look at your sinful fear because it's in doing so that you'll find the strong, loving help that you need.

"I Feared the People"—Saul

During the early history of the nation of Israel, a man named Saul became the first king. From the beginning, Saul's life was marked by fear. When Samuel the priest first went to anoint Saul as king, can you guess where he was? Was Saul in prayer, humbling himself before God? Was he out serving the people he was going to lead? No, Samuel found Saul hiding in fear amongst some wagons and carts.

Saul was afraid to do what God had called him to do. He didn't feel that he was up to the task. Certainly, taking on a position of great responsibility can be intimidating. But Saul had met with God. Samuel had also told Saul that this was God's idea…and still Saul hid. Maybe, like Adam, he foolishly thought he could hide from God and ignore His plan.

Later on, when Saul went to war against God's enemies, he gave in again to his sinful fear. On one occasion, he grew anxious when Samuel didn't come to offer prayers and sacrifices for the peoples' victory in battle, so he broke God's law and offered the sacrifices himself. On another occasion, when he was supposed to kill all of God's enemies, including the livestock, he disobeyed God because he feared the displeasure of the Israelites. Here's how he justified himself when Samuel confronted him:

- "Because I saw that the people were scattering from me...I forced myself and offered the burnt offering" (1 Samuel 13:11-12).
- "I have sinned; I have indeed transgressed the command of the Lord and your words, *because I feared the people* and listened to their voice" (1 Samuel 15:24, emphasis added).

Saul twice disobeyed God's commands because he was afraid of the people. In giving in to his fears, Saul was portraying his true thoughts about God—about whether He could be trusted, obeyed, or relied upon. Saul would never have said that he thought God was a liar or was unreliable; no, he just acted like it. The account of Saul's life is one of the saddest stories in all the Bible. In the end he committed suicide because he was afraid of what his enemies might do to him.

Saul struggled with many different fears, but mostly with *the fear of man.* This fear is a very common problem for almost everyone. It's the reason we get "butterflies" in our stomach when we have to speak in front of a crowd. It's why our hands sweat and our mouth gets dry. It's why I forgot my lines and embarrassed my classmates. The fear of man is a common problem faced by many, including many people in the Bible. Let's take a moment to look at another example, which involves the apostle Peter.

"Jesus?...I Don't Know the Man!"—Peter

Of all the characters of the New Testament, Peter is the one that I identify with most. Always ready to offer his opinion, speaking before he thinks, and confident about his fidelity, I can see that we're cut from the same cloth. He made many mistakes, but there was one particular incident that probably never ceased to bring him sorrow when he looked back upon it.

Jesus was growing more and more popular with the masses every day. It seemed as though they loved Him so much that they would make Him their king. On the other hand, the religious leaders of Israel were becoming more and more set in their hatred and envy of Him. They were determined to kill Jesus—all they had to do was find a way.

On the night Jesus was betrayed, Jesus and His friends were on their way to pray in the Garden of Gethsemane. "You will all fall away because of Me this night," He said. Peter, typically in character, remonstrated, "Even though all may fall away because of You, I will never fall away....Even if I have to die with You, I will not deny You," he claimed (Matthew 26:33,35).

We all know how this story unfolded, don't we? That night Jesus was arrested and taken away to the house of the high priest for questioning. As Peter tried to stay warm by the fires outside, a little servant girl accused him of being one of Jesus' followers. Overcome with fear, Peter said, "I do not know what you are talking about." Later another servant girl said, "This man was with Jesus of Nazareth," and this time he denied it with an oath—"I do not know the man." A little later a group of bystanders came up to him, saying, "Surely you too are one of them; for even the way you talk gives you away" (Matthew 26:73). This time Peter was determined to stop the questioning so he "began to curse and swear, 'I do not know the man!'" (Matthew 26:74). Peter's fear was so strong that it caused him to deny the Savior he loved.

The darkness of that night and his failure undoubtedly spread its gloom like a shroud over Peter's heart for three days until he heard about the resurrection. Can you imagine the torment of his soul as he recalled the goodness of his lord and the shame of his fearful actions? Can you imagine how many times he must have rehearsed his cowardly words in his mind—*I do not know the man! I do not know the man!* And then there was the look that passed between him and Jesus after the third denial. The Bible records this meaningful interchange very simply, "The Lord turned and looked at Peter" (Luke 22:61). Peter experienced the full force of the consequences of his fear, and if it weren't for the resurrection and Jesus' forgiveness and restoration, he would have never recovered. But he did recover and went on to preach before thousands and to face a martyr's death with great courage. What could change a fearful, cursing man into one who could rest, trust, and act with great heroism? Only a relationship with the living God.

Can you see how we're just like Peter and Saul? On the one hand we know that God is powerful and filled with love for us, but on the other hand we frequently find ourselves overcome by the fear of those around us. It seems that in this area particularly, we're filled with contradictions. We may neglect opportunities to witness to others or become more concerned about what our co-workers think than what God thinks. All true Christians long to have their lives shine brightly before others, but when it comes down to actually turning on the light, we frequently find ourselves hiding out like Saul or denying that we even know the Lord, like Peter. Since the fear of man is such a common and distressing snare, we're going to take a closer look at it in chapter 5.

Reluctant Cowards into Faithful Heroes

As you can see, even great Bible heroes like Abraham, Moses, and Peter weren't always characterized by great bravery. Now, I'm not saying that all of God's people were always conquered by their fears—there are enough Daniels, Shadrachs, Marys, and Pauls in Scripture to let us know that God can change hearts and lives. In that you can rejoice. But you can also take comfort in the fact that God loves to call the fearful heart to Himself. God has worked in His children's lives consistently throughout history: He's brought them peace in the midst of violent storms, courage when confronting overwhelmingly powerful enemies, and confidence in the face of accusations and persecution. He's helped them to stand before unfriendly judges and kings. He's given them the supernatural boldness to "stop the mouths of lions." If He is able to help His children in the extraordinarily difficult circumstances described in the Bible, He can give you tranquility and joy as you face the day-to-day pressures that threaten to overwhelm you.

Why does God delight in helping us to become trusting children, filled with peace and confidence, children who lean on His strength? Because when He changes hearts like ours into hearts like His, He receives praise and glory. When we discover that we're able to walk peacefully through conditions that formerly terrified us, our hearts will overflow with gratitude and thanksgiving—and that brings joy to God. Only He can change hearts that are frequently overwhelmed by fear into hearts that are overshadowed by His power and bravery, and it's His delight to do so.

For Further Thought

1. In what ways are you like Adam and Eve, Abraham and Sarah, Moses, the Israelites, Saul, and Peter?

2. How does it help you to know that well-known people in the Bible struggled in the same ways you do?

3. Do you believe that it is possible for God to change you the way that He changed others?

4. What are the fears that you have about God's work in your life?

5. What changes can you pray for right now?

3

Replacing Your Fear
with God's Power

*"The rod of God does not smite us as sharply
as the rod of our own imagination does...."*[1]

—CHARLES H. SPURGEON

$\mathcal{A}$s the operations officer of a midsized corporation, it was Gina's responsibility to oversee many of the day-to-day relationships between her employees and her company's customers. Gina had worked hard to achieve her position of authority. She had put aside her desire for a family to earn her master's degree and pursue her career. She had honed her public speaking skills to a high level. But Gina had a problem. Even though she knew that good management involved delegation and trust of others, she found it increasingly difficult to "let go." Because she felt that she couldn't trust others to do what she wanted them to do, she was overworked, stressed, and felt unappreciated. Even though she recognized that she was surrounded by capable workers, she just didn't feel that she could trust them. She was afraid that if she didn't oversee every little detail of the business it would fail, and that would mean that she was a failure as well.

Her fear also caused her to respond defensively whenever any of her subordinates suggested new ways to handle the business. Then, when anyone pointed out that she was being defensive, she responded by becoming more defensive and angry. Even though she had many friends in the company, she was becoming increasingly isolated because when her employees saw the problem and spoke with her about it, she would accuse them of disloyalty and try to push them out. She frequently couldn't sleep at night as she imagined how others probably disliked and betrayed her. Her mind painted grim pictures of life without a job, of the shame of being fired, of becoming a "bag lady" with no friends. The problem reached critical mass when her immediate supervisors told her that she had to change or suffer the consequences. She had earnestly prayed about her problem, but it seemed that every time she determined to do better, she would find herself in the women's lounge running down anyone who had criticized her to whomever would listen. Things were out of control and she was becoming more and more afraid that her job was in jeopardy.

As a Christian, Gina thought that she might have some kind of spiritual problem but she just couldn't figure out what it was. What was happening in her life? Why did she choose to handle people, even people she appreciated and valued, in negative ways? Was there any hope for her?

Gina isn't the only person who ever struggled with fear on the job. Her fear grew out of her desire to feel like she was in control. Feeling the need to control others is something that many people struggle with, particularly people who are competent and ambitious. Some people might lean more towards this kind of fear because they learned as a child that they could never rely on anyone besides themselves. Others might have too high of an opinion of themselves, thinking that everyone else is incapable. Whatever the history or cause, you know if you're a person who falls into this category and you know the stress and destruction this desire brings.

In chapter 4 we're going to look more in depth at the problems that a controlling person faces. But for now, let's just say that the desire to be in control is something that is found in people everywhere at every economic level, and gives rise to much fear.

Life would certainly be easier if our fears would remain isolated in certain areas of our lives, wouldn't it? For instance, Gina would have been happy if she could exclude her fears from her workplace. Others would be happy if they could just go to the store without having to face panic and anxiety. Unfortunately, fear (like other emotions) is not easily confined to one place or another. And God's people, as we've already seen, are likely to have very real struggles with fear. In fact, even pastors and those in the ministry struggle with fear in their pulpits and in their relationships with the members of their church. Consider the example of Timothy.

Timothy was a young disciple in the early church. The son of a Greek father and a Jewish mother who had become a Christian, Timothy was probably won to Christ through Paul's ministry. He accompanied Paul on a number of missionary endeavors and was highly spoken of by him. He was known as a man of loyalty, sensitivity, and zeal. But, he was also a man who struggled with fear.

On two different occasions, Paul specifically addresses Timothy's struggle with fear. The first is mentioned in 1 Corinthians 16:10, where Paul tells the Corinthian Christians to care for Timothy by seeing that he is "without cause to be afraid." The second appears in the book of 2 Timothy, where Paul wrote, "I want to remind you to stir into flame the strength and boldness that is in you....For the Holy Spirit, God's gift, *does not want you to be afraid...*" (2 Timothy 1:6-7 TLB, emphasis added).

It's not too much of a stretch to see that Timothy struggled with fear, or that Paul, his loving father in the faith, was concerned about how this affected Timothy's life and ministry.

Later in the same letter, Paul encouraged Timothy to "be strong in the grace that is in Christ Jesus" (2 Timothy 2:1).

God's Life-Changing Presence

In this chapter, we're going to take a closer look at Paul's advice to Timothy. We'll see how God worked in his life by filling him with His enabling strength in three specific areas: power, love, and discipline (or a sound mind). Paul knew that Timothy needed to focus on the effectiveness of God's presence in his life...and so do we. Here's what Paul said:

> I remind you to stir up the gift of God which is in you through the laying on of my hands. For God has not given us a spirit of fear, but of power and of love and of a sound mind.
> —2 Timothy 1:6-7 NKJV

Paul wanted to remind Timothy of what God had graciously given him. He had been given the "gift of God." This gifting equipped him to fulfill God's will in his life. *Well,* you might be thinking, *if the apostle Paul had prayed specifically for me, I wouldn't be afraid either.* It is true that none of us have had the personal experience with the great apostle that Timothy had, but we've got something far better. We've got the prayers of the Son of God: "He is able also to save forever those who draw near to God through Him, since He always lives to make intercession for them" (Hebrews 7:25).

You see, the Lord Jesus is praying for you, even now, as you read this book. He's graciously gifted you to fulfill the ministry He's called you to, in exactly the same way that He gifted young Timothy. You may not be called to full-time ministry or church leadership, but whatever your calling, whether it's being a mom, a student, or a corporate executive, *He has given you everything you need to fulfill it.*

In this gifting, the Lord hasn't placed in your heart an attitude of fearfulness or timidity. No, if you're a Christian, He has indwelt you with His Spirit: His *power*, His *love*, His *discipline to have a sound mind*. It's because of the indwelling character of God that Timothy, you, and I can fulfill His calling in our lives.

Let's look now at how power, love, and a sound mind fight against fear and how we can kindle afresh the gift of God in us.

God's Dynamic Power

God had given Timothy the power or courage to encounter the difficulties and dangers he would have to face. He had within him the power to bear up under trials and to triumph in persecutions. He had this power because he was indwelt by the Spirit of power—the Spirit of the God, who had all authority and power given to Him.

This power or ability to stand in the face of trouble and trials is part of God's gracious gift to His children. That's because standing for righteousness and truth is something that every Christian is called to do. So, even though you may feel weak and afraid, the truth is that the One who holds all power has made His power available to you.

Some people teach that the way to overcome fear is by trusting in yourself or building up your own self-confidence. But God doesn't want you to put your trust in your own powers or abilities. It's quite obvious, isn't it, that even at our strongest, we just aren't powerful enough? *God wants you to put your trust in His power.* Paul taught the Christians in Corinth that their faith needed to rest on the power of God (1 Corinthians 2:5).

Let's look for a moment at how powerful God's Spirit already is in our lives:

- He is more powerful than any demonic power (Matthew 12:28).

- He's powerful enough to create new life within you (John 6:63).

- God's Spirit is an eternally abiding helper (John 14:16).

- He will teach you and remind you of Jesus' words (John 14:26).

- He gives life to your mortal body (Romans 8:11).

- He leads and enables you to know with confidence that you are God's child (Romans 8:14-15).

- He assures you that you are an heir of God (Romans 8:16-17).

- The Spirit helps you in your weakness by praying for you (Romans 8:26-27).

- He's powerful enough to overcome your doubts and help you to abound in hope (Romans 15:13).

- His strong love will cause you to bow before the Lordship of Jesus (1 Corinthians 12:3).

- He gives gifts that equip you for the work God has planned for you (1 Corinthians 12:4).

- He helps you to comprehend what God has freely given to you (1 Corinthians 2:10-12).

- He is powerful enough to change you into a person who is filled with love, joy, peace, patience, kindness, goodness, faithfulness, gentleness and self-control (Galatians 5:22-23).

God's Power to Conquer Sin

The Holy Spirit lives in all of God's children and is powerful enough to accomplish the miraculous in our lives. It's this indwelling power that enables you to conquer your sinful fears. Romans 8:13 teaches that it is by this same Spirit that you can put to death the deeds of the body.[2]

On your own, in your own strength, you'll never be able to conquer your sinful fear. That's because no one is truly able to change the bent of his own nature. Sure, we can make outer changes: We can lose weight or learn to swim, but change in the heart is something that only the Holy Spirit can accomplish. The kind of change that we need—change that will free us from sin—comes from only one place: the Holy Spirit. But don't despair. If you're a Christian, His power is available to you today.

Conquering Fearful Imaginations

As I drove on the freeway on my way to church, I struggled with a fear that many grandmothers know. My daughter was about to give birth to our first grandchild, and in my imagination she had died in childbirth. In fact, not only had she died, but our grandchild had died with her, and I pictured them laying together in a coffin. I had no logical reason to think these thoughts, for my daughter and her baby were well, but this imagination was as real in my mind as if it had actually happened. I wept. I tried to imagine life after this tragedy. *How could I go on?* I thought that I should turn my car around and head home because I certainly couldn't go to church in this condition. Then, the Holy Spirit convicted me: *What was I doing?* I was allowing my imagination to frighten and terrify me. I knew instantly that what I was doing was wrong, so I asked God's forgiveness. I prayed,

> *God, only You know what will happen in my future. You hold my life in Your hand. I know that You haven't promised that I'll never suffer loss, but You have promised to uphold me if, in Your loving plan, I must. Please help me to rejoice in You and put my whole trust in You. Amen.*

After that I turned on a praise tape and focused my thoughts and imagination on worshiping and blessing God. I was now ready to go to church.

You know, the problem with fears that exist only in our imagination is that, since they aren't real, we must face them alone. God's grace isn't available to help us overcome imaginary problems that reside only in our mind. He will help us to put these imagined fears to death, but it's only in the *real world* that His power is effective to uphold us in trouble. It's only when He calls us to actually *go through difficult times* that His power is present to protect, comfort, and strengthen us.

During the Second World War, God raised up a family of Dutch Christians who helped to hide Jewish people from the advancing German armies. This awe-inspiring story of sacrifice and courage is told in the book *The Hiding Place*, and is written by the only surviving daughter of the family, Corrie ten Boom.

As a young girl, Corrie came face to face with her own fears. A neighbor's baby had died and Corrie realized that it was possible for anyone to die, even her own beloved father. "You can't die! You can't!" she sobbed. This is how she described her father's response to her fear:

> Father sat down on the edge of the narrow bed. "Corrie," he began gently, "when you and I go to Amsterdam—when do I give you your ticket?"
>
> I sniffed a few times, considering this.
>
> "Why, just before we get on the train."
>
> "Exactly. And our wise Father in heaven knows when we're going to need things, too. Don't run ahead of Him, Corrie. When the time comes that some of us will have to die, you will look into your heart and find the strength you need—just in time."[3]

Can you see what Corrie's father was teaching her? When God calls you to face something frightening, whether it's your own death, a tragedy in the family, or some other difficulty, it is then, *and only then,* that He provides you with the strength to live through it. Over the years I've tried to remember that I don't need the "ticket" of God's strength and grace for a train that hasn't, or may never, arrive. The only ticket I need is for the train that I have to board right now, and God has promised to provide that ticket for me when I need it. "I will never leave you nor forsake you," He has said to us (Hebrews 13:5 NKJV). That means that He'll be there, holding our hand, no matter what train He has called into the station.

Fear that exists in our imagination is a formidable foe. But it can be put to death by the Spirit and faith. The great English preacher Charles Spurgeon once preached a sermon on needless fears. Here's a portion of what he said:

> ...many of God's people are constantly under apprehensions of calamities which will never occur to them, and they suffer far more in merely dreading them than they would have to endure if they actually came upon them. In their imagination, there are rivers in their way, and they are anxious to know how they shall wade through them, or swim across them. There are no such rivers in existence, but they are agitated and distressed about them...these timid people are continually crossing bridges that only exist in their...fancies. They stab themselves with imaginary daggers, they starve themselves in imaginary famines, and even bury themselves in imaginary graves....[4]

As we continue through this book we'll see how the Holy Spirit can help us control our thoughts and learn to discipline our minds. For now, though, it is important that we begin to see how our sinful imagination feeds our fears.

Developing a Sound Mind

In 2 Timothy 1:6-7, Paul mentioned three things God had given to Timothy: power, love, and discipline (or a sound mind). In chapter 10 we will cover love, so for now we'll focus on one of the results of the Spirit's power: a sound mind.

Paul advised Timothy to remember that God had given him the ability to discipline his mind. The word that Paul used here is used only once in the New Testament, and refers to the faculty of mind that enables one to control his thoughts, to be of sound mind. The point is that God had given Timothy the ability or capacity to have a disciplined, sound mind. A sound mind is one that is quietly focused on truth: first the truth about who God is and what He has said, and second, the truth about ourselves.

What is your mind focused on? Just about all of us struggle with fears that can lead our mind to flit from one possible disaster to another. We can dream up a worst-case scenario in seconds; our thoughts are filled with graphic images of illness, death, disaster, or troubles. Rather than focusing on the goodness and strength of God, we focus on impending disasters, with God coming only as an afterthought. It may even be that the thoughts that occupy your mind are so strong that you forget about God completely. It's easy to see that the discipline of developing a sound mind is something we all need to cultivate.

Undisciplined imaginations are the cause of discouragement and anxiety. When I was filled with fearful imaginations about my daughter and grandchild, I wasn't disciplining my mind or thinking about the truth. My mind was anything but quiet! A sound mind is a mind that can enjoy peace even in the midst of a great storm because it is anchored in what's really true. In the Old Testament, the prophet Isaiah spoke of this quietness of mind: "The steadfast of mind You will keep in perfect peace, *because he trusts in You*" (Isaiah 26:3, emphasis added).

The Stability in Trusting God

Perfect peace is available only to the one whose mind is steadfastly fixed on trusting God. What does it mean to "trust" in God? *Trust* is the result of a *decision to choose to believe* that God is worthy of our confidence, reliance, faith, and dependence.

Trust in God grows only as we become more and more acquainted with Him—with His power, His goodness, and His wisdom. Trust blooms in the heart that has come to believe that "God in His love always wills what is best for us. In His wisdom He always knows what is best, and in His sovereignty He has the power to bring it about."[5] As I grow in my comprehension of God's love, wisdom, and sovereign power, my trust in Him and ability to refute vain imaginations grow as well.

Many people who struggle with fear do so because, for whatever reason, they've learned that they can't trust others. Some people think that they'll never be able to really trust God because they've experienced great betrayal, difficulty, or shame. But the freeing truth is that God never tells us that we need to trust people. In fact, He commands just the opposite:

- "It is better to take refuge in the Lord than to trust in man. It is better to take refuge in the Lord than to trust in princes" (Psalm 118:8-9).
- "Do not trust in princes, in mortal man, in whom there is no salvation" (Psalm 146:3).
- "Cursed is the man who trusts in mankind" (Jeremiah 17:5).

Of course, as we live our day-to-day lives, we have to trust people to some extent. I have to trust that the checker at the grocery store isn't purposely trying to steal from me. I have to trust that when the traffic light turns red, oncoming traffic will stop so that I can go through the intersection. This is trust, but it's a measured trust. It isn't a trust that says, "Everything depends on you." In the face of my measured trust I acknowledge that it is possible that the checker is trying to steal from me, so I glance at my receipts. I also know that there are people who habitually run red lights, so I look both ways even when I have a green light. I have a measured trust that people will do what they should, but I also understand that people sin and make mistakes, and so I try not to be foolish.

The Evidence of God's Trustworthiness

God doesn't want or expect us to have *blind* trust in anyone—not even in Himself. As our Creator, He has every right to command that we trust in Him without giving us any clues as to His trustworthiness. But He hasn't done that. In the Bible, He has revealed everything about Himself that we need to know. He has shown through creation, history, and our redemption that He's fully trustworthy. It's as we grow in our trust of Him—of His wisdom, love, and sovereign power—that we'll find our fears fading away. When this happens, we'll also be able to trust others as we should.

When it comes to the focus of my life, to my peace of mind, my deepest joy, or my ability to serve the Lord, it's impossible that I should trust anyone other than Him. Not only would it be foolish for me to trust others in this way, but doing so would dishonor God. One person observed, "We cannot expect God to prosper anything which intrudes itself into His place, and detracts from His honour....[We must] make God the great object of our trust, *even though the usual human instrumentality of help may be at hand.*"[6]

Peace in God's Presence

Even though it may seem that your life is filled with troubles and trials, you can begin today to know the peace of God. Even though you may have known great disappointment, disloyalty, or bitter despair, the peace that Jesus gives is for *all* His children. This peace is something we'll talk about a lot in upcoming chapters, but for now, meditate on these words from Jesus:

> Peace I leave with you; My peace I give to you; not as the world gives do I give to you. Do not let your heart be troubled, nor let it be fearful.
>
> —John 14:27

When Paul reminded Timothy that God had not given him a spirit of fear, perhaps he was remembering the kind of fear that the Israelites had at Mount Sinai, when they asked Moses to meet God for them. Paul was encouraging Timothy not to be like those people, who, when they saw the nearness of God, fled in fear. And God is calling to each of us today not to run from Him in slavish fear, but instead to draw near to Him with humble, trusting hearts, letting His peace flood over our souls. We can know joyful serenity as we experience the gentle care of His fatherly guidance, the astonishing love seen in His Son's sacrifice, and the reassuring power of His transforming Spirit. And it all comes down to trusting God.

For Further Thought

Trust in God is something that we must strive for. As a loving Father, He grants us enough understanding of His nature so that we can come to Him. But growing in this trust is something we must choose to do. We can do so by considering what He has said about Himself and those who trust in Him. As we close this chapter, take time to prayerfully meditate on the following verses:

- "Lord, there is no one besides You to help in the battle between the powerful and those who have no strength; so help us, O Lord our God, for we trust in You" (2 Chronicles 14:11).

- "Those who know your name will put their trust in You, for You, O Lord, have not forsaken those who seek You" (Psalm 9:10).

- "In You our fathers trusted; they trusted and You delivered them. To You they cried out and were delivered; in You they trusted and were not disappointed" (Psalm 22:4-5).

- "The Lord is my strength and my shield; my heart trusts in Him, and I am helped" (Psalm 28:7).

- "Trust in Him at all times, O people; pour out your heart before Him; God is a refuge for us" (Psalm 62:8).

- "God is my salvation, I will trust and not be afraid; for the Lord GOD is my strength and song, and He has become my salvation" (Isaiah 12:2).

- "Trust in the Lord forever, for in GOD the Lord, we have an everlasting Rock" (Isaiah 26:4).

- "In repentance and rest you will be saved, in quietness and trust is your strength" (Isaiah 30:15).

More excellent verses you can study include 1 Chronicles 5:20; 2 Chronicles 13:18; 20:20; Psalm 13:5; 32:10; 37:5; 40:4; 84:12; 112:7; 115:11; Proverbs 28:25; 29:25.

4

When You Feel
You're Losing Control

*"Yours is the mighty power and glory and victory
and majesty. Everything in the heavens and earth is yours,
O Lord, and this is your kingdom. We adore you
as being in control of everything."*

—1 CHRONICLES 29:11 TLB

*I*f we had a choice between being able to control our circumstances and having no control over them, I'm sure everyone would go for the first option. We would much rather that life be like a peaceful stroll by a gentle stream, but usually it more closely resembles a wild toboggan ride down a steep snow-covered hill, and the further along we go, the more anxious we are that we won't be able to stop without the intervention of a tree. For those of us who struggle with wanting to be in control of our circumstances, the situations where we feel vulnerable and helpless can be absolutely terrifying.

As I write this, I'm anticipating a plane trip across the country. Flying in airplanes has never been terribly frightening for me personally, but I know plenty of people who worry and fret about it for days beforehand. Statistically, flying is a pretty safe mode of travel; in fact, it's safer than driving a car. But the reality is that flying *is* scarier than driving a car. Why? Because when we're cruising down the freeway at 65 miles per hour, we're under the impression that we're in control of our personal safety. We foolishly assume that if something unexpected were to happen, we could respond to it and keep ourselves from harm. But when we're flying and we feel unexpected turbulence or the pilot suddenly throttles back, we experience the insecurity of being vulnerable to another's control. We're more comfortable driving because we're more in control than we are in an airplane. It's this feeling of being in control of our own safety that we relish.

Wanting to Be in Control

Gina, the executive we met in the last chapter, strongly believed that she needed to be in control. This desire to control the events surrounding her life created all sorts of problems for her: she was angry, worried, burned out, and difficult to get along with. Gina recognized that she was exhausting herself by trying to be in control of everything—but she was afraid to stop! She felt that her life was racing at breakneck speed toward a frighteningly unpredictable future. These feelings of insecurity caused her to exert more and more effort to get things back into control. She did this because she thought that if she didn't, she was doomed. She was afraid for her career. She was afraid that her life would fall apart. And then, in an ever-increasing downward spiral, the more fearful she became about her need to be in control, the more she attempted to dominate her employees and circumstances, which created even more problems for herself. Gina was wearing herself out and she was wearing out her friendships as well. What was going on in Gina's heart that caused her to be so controlling? Did God understand her struggles? Could He help her?

Then there was Dottie, who became a Christian as an adult after living a rather wild life. She had been rebellious and angry as a young person. After Christ marvelously saved her, she married and birthed three children she was "raising for the Lord." She devoted her energies to trying to control her children's behavior in part because she was afraid that they might grow up and be rebellious like she had been. To those in her church she had a reputation for being a good mom because she was involved in her children's schooling and she devoted herself to her family. But she was known by her children as a woman who had a temper, whom they had better not cross. She recognized that her anger was sinful and she wanted to be free from it, but she was confused. Why did she feel angry all the time? She didn't understand that much of her anger was fear-based. After all, she simply wanted to protect her kids from making the same mistakes that she had made. She was going to make sure that they would serve the Lord. Indeed, her children were learning how to say all the right "Christian" words, how to act in church, and how to please Mom. But they were also learning how to be angry and afraid. No one could have accused Dottie of not loving her children. She did love them and wanted the best for them. Dottie's problem wasn't a lack of love; rather, her problem was fear. Dottie needed help, and so did her family.

A Downward Spiral

Along with these and many other disturbing thoughts and yearnings that are brought about by fear, there is yet something else that causes people to want to feel "in control." It is itself the result of fear, anxiety, or panic: a panic attack. This can be a very frightening experience. In an attack, fear, panic, and anxiety produce very uncomfortable and powerful symptoms that may include a racing heart, lightheadedness, and even nausea.

As we saw in chapter 1, these physical responses are part of God's loving design to help us respond to danger. God designed the body to experience discomfort when adrenaline is released into the bloodstream so that we would be motivated to respond quickly to perceived danger. The desire to be free of these uncomfortable symptoms is also natural. It's just the question of *how we get free* that is so difficult. It is difficult because our physical responses are not directly within our control. In other words, it doesn't matter how much we tell ourselves not to be afraid or that we aren't going to have another panic attack. In fact, the more we focus on trying to overcome the possibility, the more likely we are to have another one. It becomes obvious quickly that this isn't a problem that we're going to be able to ignore or talk ourselves out of.

Another way that those who have suffered from panic attacks try to control their occurrence is to avoid places where the attacks have happened. Remember Kathryn, who was afraid of being sick at the mall? To avoid the possibility of having another attack, she had simply stopped going there.

One woman shared with me a very specific fear she had while driving: On a particularly busy freeway there is a fork where the freeway divides into two. After having felt panicky when approaching the fork, she had become increasingly more afraid that she wouldn't be able to choose between the two. She was afraid her fear might paralyze her and she would end up crashing into the divider. She had never had trouble making the choice before, but eventually this fear became so enslaving that she refused to drive on this freeway again, even though it made getting around in her town very difficult. Her fear of the panic and how she might respond to it became an enslaving tyrant which was cutting off more and more of her outside world. This put her into a downward spiral, which led to a continually worsening fear and desire to control her circumstances.

Here's how this downward spiral might look:

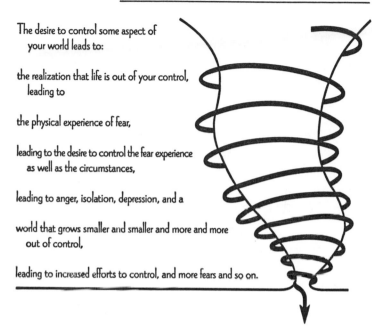

The desire to control some aspect of your world leads to:

the realization that life is out of your control, leading to

the physical experience of fear,

leading to the desire to control the fear experience as well as the circumstances,

leading to anger, isolation, depression, and a

world that grows smaller and smaller and more and more out of control,

leading to increased efforts to control, and more fears and so on.

Why do people live this way? What's really at the heart of this problem? Does the Bible speak to these issues?

The Prophet Who Wanted to Be in Charge

Gina and Dottie remind me of a man in the Bible named Jonah. Jonah was a prophet who lived in Old Testament times. God had called him to go to the ungodly city of Nineveh and preach to them about the judgment that God was about to bring upon them. But instead of obeying God's commands, Jonah ran away. You've heard the story about how God exercised control over Jonah by sending a storm and a great fish, but have you ever wondered why Jonah responded in the way that he did to God's bidding?

We don't have to speculate about Jonah's motivation because the Bible gives us the answer. After Jonah reluctantly preached to the Ninevites, God saw their deeds and He "relented concerning the calamity which He had declared He would bring upon them" (Jonah 3:10). Jonah's desire to be in charge of the outcome of his ministry is seen in his response to God's mercy. He said, "Please Lord, was not this what I said while I was still in my own country? Therefore *in order to forestall this I fled to Tarshish*" (4:2, emphasis added). Jonah was angry that God didn't punish the Ninevites after he preached to them. Why? Because Jonah wanted to be *in charge*. He was afraid to look foolish and he cared more about how he looked and his own success than he did about God's compassion for the people. Jonah disobeyed God because he wanted to be in control.

The story of Jonah displays God's great love. It's a story about His great love for the Ninevites and His powerful love for His servant, Jonah. In the last scene in this book, we see God continuing to lovingly instruct Jonah about his wrong thinking and desires. Let me remind you of it: After Jonah had preached to the Ninevites, he went up on a hill to watch and see what God would do. The day was hot, and as Jonah camped out under a little shelter he had made, God caused a plant to grow up over him that protected him from the heat. The Bible says that Jonah was very happy about the plant. He probably thought that God was bringing this comfort to him because he'd done such a good job of preaching. But then God "appointed a worm" to destroy the plant. Next, He sent a "scorching east wind," and "the sun beat down on Jonah's head." This made Jonah very uncomfortable and angry. Why was God now bringing this discomfort into Jonah's life? Was God angry with Jonah? Was He punishing him? No, God loved Jonah and sought to instruct him. What was God teaching Jonah? *God was teaching Jonah who He was. He was teaching him that He was in control. He was opening Jonah's blind eyes so that he could see the flaws in his thinking that caused him to be so disobedient, angry, and unhappy.*

Jonah was inappropriately focused on the *outcome* of his ministry "for God." He wanted to control how people responded.

Why? He wanted to look good. He wanted to see God's enemies punished. He wanted to be the "man in charge." He wanted to usurp God's role, being in control. Jonah didn't have the courage, compassion, and patience that he needed because he wasn't focused on the greatness of God. He had lost sight of God's compassion. Jonah was concerned about losing *his* comfort, *his* happiness, and *his* reputation rather than the eternal happiness of the more than 120,000 people in Nineveh. Even though Jonah had been delivered from the prison of the great fish that swallowed him, he was still imprisoned by his cravings to be in charge...and these cravings caused Jonah to fear.

Like Jonah, those who are mastered by their fears might find themselves in very cramped quarters: Surrounded by darkness, wrapped in cold, feeling isolated and alone. Or they might wonder why God keeps stirring up their nest so that they can never feel really comfortable, really in charge. They wonder if God is angry, or if He loves them. They wonder, *What's He up to?*

Please don't misunderstand what I'm saying about Jonah. I'm not saying that he didn't love God. In fact, he admitted to the sailors who tossed him overboard that he was a man who feared God. And like Jonah, many of us see within ourselves two competing desires: yes, we love God and want to serve Him. But there is also the desire to control people and events for our own purposes, to calm our fears.

It's a Matter of Trust

Perhaps there is within our hearts a subtle desire to try to control God. Perhaps we think that God isn't really in charge or that He is too far away or too busy to get involved in our day-to-day lives. Is it possible that we don't really yet understand how much He loves us or how powerful He is? We might misinterpret our experience with the great fish or the worm that eats our comfortable shade as a lack of love, wisdom, or power on God's part. Life seems chaotic and unpredictable.

And finally, perhaps, we don't really believe that He's trust-worthy, so we work harder and harder trying to bring life back under our control.

You see, the desire to control people or circumstances is, at heart, a *trust problem*. Hopefully, it's not that we don't trust God for our initial salvation. Rather, it's that we don't trust Him to work things out for our good. We think that we have to do that. We find it almost impossible to let go of those things that are most dear to us: our children, our careers, our future. And so, when God brings a fish or a worm to get our attention, we automatically think that's because He isn't able to control our circumstances or that He's unhappy with us.

Think about the trials or difficulties that you are facing. Per-haps your children are rebellious, or your new boss is a tyrant. Perhaps your best friend is moving out of the state, or you've just found out that you need major surgery. Is it possible that God has allowed these specific difficulties into your life to teach you of His goodness, of your inability to control events, and to set you free from your fears? We're going to learn more about how to interpret our trials in the light of God's character in Part Three of this book. But for now, ask yourself what it is that God might be trying to teach you or free you from, even in the experience of your fears. The trials that you face are not the result of God's powerlessness; they're a sign of His loving care.

Yielding Control to God

At the opening of this chapter I quoted 1 Chronicles 29:11, which reads, "Yours is the mighty power and glory and vic-tory and majesty. Everything in the heavens and earth is yours, O Lord, and this is your kingdom. We adore you as being in control of everything" (TLB).

Think for a moment about the words "we adore you as being in control of everything." You know, when we really stop to think about it, we are forced to recognize that all our efforts at controlling our world are pretty ineffective, aren't they? In fact, we have to recognize that there is only one person who is really in control—and that's God. We'll talk more about God's control, what the Bible calls His *sovereign rule*, in chapter 8, but I do want to bring up this important point: *God is already in charge, and whenever we try to be, we're God-playing.* We're trying to be like a god rather than being Godlike.

Challenging God's Control

Where did this desire to be in control, to be like a god, originally come from? It had its birth in the Garden of Eden. Do you remember how Satan tempted Eve? He said, "God knows that when you eat from [the fruit] your eyes will be opened, and *you will be like God*" (Genesis 3:5, emphasis added). Think about that phrase "you will be like God." What was Satan saying to Eve? He was saying, "You can't trust God. He hasn't given you everything you really need. He isn't trustworthy…He doesn't really love you…you need to be afraid that you're going to miss out…so go ahead, disobey God. Take matters into your own hands, try to work things out in accordance to your own wisdom. You need to be in control. Then you'll be happy."

It's a blessing that God doesn't let this kind of thinking go on for long, isn't it? It wasn't long until God visited Adam and Eve and found them hiding in shame. He didn't let Jonah spend any time in Tarshish, but instead brought loving correction in the form of a storm and a large fish. God continues today to lovingly confront us whenever we give in to the temptation of trying to be in control. He does this for our own good and so that He'll be praised.

Pursuing Our Own Control

When we spend our lives pursuing sinful control over our world, we find that our world does something amazing—it shrinks! Instead of growing stronger and becoming people who have grand hearts and great capacities for loving obedience, our hearts become small, darkened, and frightened, and we find ourselves trembling in the cold. We become like Jonah, who didn't like God's choice to spare Nineveh, and we become like Eve, who thought that in order to be happy she had to control her own future. As a result she could no longer live in a beautiful garden under the rule of a loving God, but was sent out to wander in the wilderness of her folly.

When we seek to be like a god in this way, we're acting just like our enemy, the devil. He wanted to be in control; he wanted to usurp God's authority. It is true that we are to be like God in other ways, in particular, in the quality of His character. We are to be holy, loving, kind, long-suffering, just, and self-controlled. But we are never called to be like Him in the qualities that He hasn't shared with us—His omnipresence, omniscience, and omnipotence. So God does command us to be like Him—after all, we are created in His image—but we must be careful to differentiate between the qualities that belong to God alone and those He has shared with us.

When God commanded Adam and Eve to rule over the world that He had created and to have dominion, He was letting them in on a portion of His rulership. So on one hand, God commanded our first parents to be in control of certain things, but all the while they needed to understand that they were merely deputies, not ruling kings. He had given them authority to rule over some things, but their rulership was always to be in submission to His. They were to obey Him by ruling, not rule in disobedience.

Because of Adam and Eve's sin, this God-given desire to control has been warped. Now we seek to control people's hearts, the outcome of events, and our future. We do this because we're afraid of what might happen if we just trust and obey.

When We Become Afraid

During His earthly ministry, Jesus told a parable or story about a man who was fearful. In this story, found in Matthew

25:14-30, Jesus likened the kingdom of heaven to a man who was about to go on a journey and called his servants to himself, entrusting them with his possessions. The Bible uses the word "talents" to describe units of money, but for the sake of simplicity, let's change this to dollars. To one servant he gave $5,000, to another he gave $2,000 and then to another $1,000, each according to their ability. After the householder left, each of the servants did something different with the money. The ones who had received $5,000 and $2,000 both wisely invested their money to make more money. The one who had received $1,000 hid it in the ground. After some time the master returned from his journey and asked for an accounting. The first two had doubled their investment and received rewards for doing so. The last one, however, merely brought back the $1,000 originally entrusted to him by his master. When questioned as to why he hadn't invested the money, the servant said, "Master, I knew you to be a hard man, reaping where you did not sow and gathering where you scattered no seed. And I was afraid, and went away and hid your talent in the ground. See, you have what is yours" (25:24-25). Can you see how the servant's perspective of his master colored his use of his gifts? Look at the words the servant used to describe his master. He said that he was hard and unreasonable. Is it true that our heavenly Master is hard and unreasonable? Do you see how this servant's view of God caused him to be afraid and made him hide his "talents" away?

Think about Jonah's and Eve's views of God. Weren't they saying essentially the same thing? Weren't they saying that the reason that they were fearful—the reason that they didn't do what God had commanded—was somehow God's fault? Don't we do the same thing when we become afraid and hide away? *But God, we think, if You had given me the strength, or intelligence, or family, or whatever...that Your other servants have, I would gladly work hard for You.*

I have seen the very same problem in my own life. When I find myself afraid, when I look at the future and I have the feeling that everything is on the verge of collapse, I find myself wanting to hide—to be self-indulgent—to go play. I know this is how I respond sometimes. It's not that I purposely squander the gifts that God has given me, it's just that I don't use them the way that I should. I just hide them away and think, *Well, God, if You weren't so hard...if You hadn't given me such a difficult life, I wouldn't be so discouraged.* Sometimes I don't want to work hard or risk obedience because I fear the result. I think that if I live my way I'll be able to control the results. I might not like the way my life is shaping up right now, but at least I know what to expect and I don't have to fear the unknown, or put my life in the hands of a God who sometimes seems hard and unreasonable.

Salvation Is from the Lord

When Jonah found himself surrounded on all sides by the reality that it was God who was really in control, he prayed this prayer:

> While I was fainting away, I remembered the LORD,
> And my prayer came to You, into Your holy temple.
> Those who regard vain idols forsake their faithfulness,
> But I will sacrifice to You with the voice of thanksgiving.
> That which I have vowed I will pay. Salvation is from the LORD."
> —Jonah 2:7-9

Let's look more closely at what Jonah was saying: First he recognized that he was in a terrible situation; he was dying. There was no escape for him; he was completely helpless. Then he "remembered the LORD." Isn't that interesting? Do you think that Jonah really forgot the Lord? Or did he just forget who the Lord was? In the original Hebrew text the word "LORD" is

Yahweh, which is the Hebrew name that God gave Himself. We know this name means not only that He is the self-existent one, but also the one *who performs all His will.*[1] Jonah knew God by this name and was saying, in essence, "You're the only one who lives eternally and You're the only one who can control the universe. You're my only hope." It was this God that Jonah remembered in the fish's belly.

He goes on to pray, "And my prayer came to You, into Your holy temple." Jonah knew that God was a prayer-hearing God. God's ability to hear wasn't obstructed by the cramped space where Jonah found himself. No, God could hear Jonah's prayer in His temple, just as though Jonah were standing right there himself, instead of in the depths of the ocean.

"Those who regard vain idols forsake their faithfulness" is the next phrase in his desperate prayer. What did Jonah mean? That he had come to the realization that clinging to any worthless idol would cause him to forfeit the grace that could be his. He knew that he had lost out on God's grace because he had been clinging to worthless idols: He had been hanging on to the belief that he was in control of his own life. In actuality, he was God-playing. Because he was trying so hard to be God, he lost out on the grace that God gives only to those who trust in Him.

"I will sacrifice to You with the voice of thanksgiving" was Jonah's new resolve. You know, we might have the tendency to read over that sentence and think, *What's the big deal? He gave thanks to God...so what?* But stop and think about where Jonah was. He wasn't standing in church on Sunday morning surrounded by people who loved God. No, he was surrounded by dark waters, seaweed had wrapped itself around him, his air supply was limited. And it was here, in the fish's belly, that he decided to worship God. He lifted up his voice in thanks from the depths of the ocean because he believed that God would hear him and that He was worthy to be praised, even if it was with his dying breath. Jonah vowed that he would be faithful to God.

Jonah then acknowledged that salvation, any salvation that might come to him, was only from the Lord. He realized that he was utterly unable to save himself. He wasn't in control. He was totally helpless. As one commentator writes,

> Salvation is still of him, as it has always been; from him alone it is to be expected, and on him we are to depend for it. Jonah's experience shall encourage others, in all ages, to trust in God as the God of their salvation; all that read this story shall say with assurance, say with admiration, that salvation is of the Lord, and is sure to all that belongs to him.[2]

Looking to God in Prayer

As we close this chapter, let me encourage you that you can pray just like Jonah did. I can't imagine a more difficult, hopeless circumstance than the one in which Jonah found himself. Revisit his predicament in your mind: the sights, the smells, the freezing wetness. And in just the same way as Jonah, even from the depths of the earth, you can call out to God and know that He will hear and answer you.

Although Jonah's prayer from that frightening place was undoubtedly sincere, he still continued to struggle with his habitual desire to be in control. Later in the story we find him struggling again with his fear. The heart that's filled with fear will continue to grasp for control. And in turn, the person who wants to be in charge will always be afraid that he's losing control. The following diagram shows the cycle of fear and desire that Jonah knew (and many of us know as well):

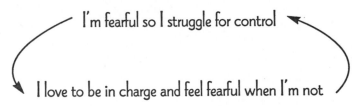

Prayer is effective and God can and does work mightily in response to it, but He usually lets us wrestle with our habitual fears for a season. That's because He wants us to grow to hate them and to desire to be free from them for the right reason: His glory. Jonah's prayer was sincere, but he had to continue to learn that God was in charge and that he could trust Him. Our growth in bold trust is something that God is in charge of. Don't misunderstand; I do believe that deliverance is possible. I've seen God change people, but this usually is a very slow process. I'm saying this because I don't want you to become discouraged if you find yourself wrapped in seaweed again or grumbling because you can't control your circumstances. God is in charge of every part of your life, even your freedom from fear. You can rest in Him and trust that His deliverance will be right on time.

Gina, Dottie, and Jonah all faced significant difficulties, didn't they? These difficulties were caused in part by their responses to the situations they found themselves in. These situations didn't create their fears and desires; rather, they served to reveal the desires that resided in their hearts already. Don't be discouraged if you see that the desire for control resides in your heart as well. God is the same today as He was in Jonah's time. He's still continuing to work out His perfect plan, and He will finish the work in you that He has promised. In response to His faithfulness, you can come to Him today, right now, in prayer and ask Him to deliver you from all your fears. The psalmist put it this way: "I sought the Lord, and He answered me, and delivered me from all my fears" (Psalm 34:4).

Take a few moments now to do the exercises below...and pray with Jonah, "Salvation is only from you, O Lord...and I believe that salvation is for me."

For Further Thought

1. Read Christ's parable of the fearful servant found in Matthew 25:14-30.

2. Do you think that there is any likeness between the fearful servant and yourself? If so, what is the similarity?

3. How does your perspective on the character of God impact your fear? The Bible commentator Matthew Henry writes this of the fearful servant: "Good thoughts of God would beget love, and that love would make us diligent and faithful; but hard thoughts of God beget fear, and that fear makes us slothful and unfaithful."[3]

4. What does the phrase "salvation is from the Lord" mean to you in your circumstances?

5. Take time now to review Jonah's prayer. Rewrite it in your own words. Remember, God is the same today as He was in Jonah's time. It's His delight to deliver you from fear and set you free so that you can serve Him with joy.

Fearing the People
Around Us

*"Regarding other people, our problem is that we **need** them
(for ourselves) more than we **love** them (for the glory of God)."*[1]
—EDWARD T. WELCH
Biblical counselor, author, and teacher

*N*icole came to me because she was struggling with the beginnings of panic attacks. She had been gifted with a beautiful voice and had enjoyed singing in church and at special meetings. Recently she had become concerned because she was becoming more and more fearful about her singing engagements. She would worry for days beforehand, afraid that once she started singing she would forget the words (something she had never done before). She was afraid that she would become so fearful that she would faint in front of the audience. She felt tormented by questions of what might happen if she was unable to go on. She was tempted to cancel all her performances.

As we talked it became apparent that like Jonah, Nicole was a mixture of fear and faith. She believed that God had gifted her to sing and that she had an obligation to use her talents for the Lord. She also believed that she had an obligation to practice, to pursue excellence in her gifting, and to seek to bring glory to God. These were not just passing thoughts to her, but were heartfelt commitments.

On the other hand, she knew that she was strongly tied to what others thought. She longed to hear that people enjoyed her performances. She discovered that she would subtly position herself to get compliments. Sometimes she would deliberately criticize herself so that others would flatter her in response. At other times she would compliment another singer in hopes that she would be told again how talented she was. She hated the fact that she felt so tied to what others said, but still she longed to hear praise. Sometimes after a performance she would berate herself for days, especially if she didn't receive the compliments she longed for. As a result, singing was becoming a terrible burden and trial for her.

How should Nicole think about her problem? Was she simply struggling with poor self-esteem? Did she need to reaffirm herself more? What would God say to her?

Loving the Praise of Man

An Old Testament Example

The Bible is filled with people who longed to hear words of praise. In the Old Testament story of Esther we are introduced to one man who really struggled with this desire. His name was Haman.

Haman was in a position of great power and authority in the ancient Persian kingdom where Ahasuerus ruled. As second in command to the king, Haman held extraordinary power over the lives of the Jews, who had been exiled from Israel. Haman was so powerful that all the people had been commanded to bow down and pay homage to him whenever he walked through the streets of the city. All the king's servants obeyed this command except one: a Jew named Mordecai. Mordecai refused to bow down or worship any human. He believed that he should worship only God. When Haman saw that Mordecai refused to bow down to him, he was "filled with rage" (Esther 3:5). Even though Haman had the praise and adulation of everyone in the kingdom, it wasn't enough. So he set out to punish Mordecai for disrespecting him. In order to do this he developed an elaborate scheme that would ultimately involve the destruction of all the Jews. But in God's sovereign plan, Haman's plan was defeated and Haman himself was killed on the gallows that he had constructed for Mordecai.

As I have thought about Haman and his desire for the praise and adulation of others, I can see how I am, in some ways, just like him. I too long to hear the praise of others; I have wondered why I don't get it from some people. My desire to hear the applause of others sometimes motivates me to be angry, fearful, and even to sin against others. I haven't actually thought about harming anyone who refused to compliment me, but I have to admit that my love for those people isn't what it should be.

A New Testament Example

In the New Testament we find other people who struggled with Haman's malady. For example, there were the Jewish believers who had come to Christ but were afraid to tell others about their conversion. This is how the New Testament describes their dilemma:

> Nevertheless many even of the rulers believed in Him, but because of the Pharisees they were not confessing Him, for fear that they would be put out of the synagogue; for they loved the approval of men rather than the approval of God.
> —John 12:42-43

Some of the Jewish religious leaders had come to faith in Christ. They knew that He was the Messiah and they had seen the truth of His claims. But they had a problem: They knew that if they confessed their faith, they would be excommunicated—they would be put out of the synagogue. I'm sure you can imagine how difficult their situation was. The synagogue, for the ancient Jew, was not like the modern church is today. Today if our beliefs conflict with our church's, we can easily pack up and move elsewhere. But that's not how it was for them. They had one synagogue, and they had an obligation to support it. All of their social and economic life was tied to the associations in the group. If they were put out of the synagogue, they were, in essence, put out of every social and business relationship in their life.

Notice that John doesn't say that their problem was one of poor self-esteem or feelings of inferiority. No, he pinpoints their problem as being a *problem of love*. What did they love more than the approval of God? The approval of man. What did they long for more than the praise that would come to them from God: "Well done, good and faithful servant"? They loved the praise of their peers. In fact, they loved it so much that they disobeyed Christ's command to witness for Him.

The word "loved" in John 12:42-43 is a very strong Greek word, *agapao*. This word is frequently used to speak of God's love for us and the kind of love that we are to have for one another. This isn't a word that meant that they "liked" hearing compliments or "liked" being popular. No, this was a word that meant that they lived for and were addicted to the approval of men.

Our Response to Criticism

Learning from Criticism

How can I tell when I've got an excessive love for what others say about me? I can tell by the ways that I respond when I'm criticized. As any author will tell you, it's difficult to hear criticism about your work. Recently I read a review of one of my books that was troubling to me. I could tell that the person who had written the review probably was not a Christian because my discussion of sin was offensive. But that didn't really matter to me at the time. I didn't like being criticized.

As I thought about this person's criticism, my first response was to hide. Remember the third servant in the story of the fearful servant in the last chapter? That's usually my first response. I think, *Okay, fine. Why should I put myself out here on the firing line? I don't need this. I'll just hide away any little talent that I might have and then I won't have to take any heat.* I usually end this tirade by saying something in my heart like, *I'll show them. If they don't appreciate what I have to say, then that's okay with me. I don't need them anyway.*

As a result, I will feel angry, fearful, and distressed. The peace and joy that Christ promises to me is nowhere to be found. I act more like Jonah, sinking down into the depths of despair. After this initial response, I usually end up thinking that I don't care what others think and that I will simply ignore them. *They're stupid anyway,* I will think. But still, there will be a nagging at the back of my mind: *Someone doesn't like you. They aren't praising your work.* In many ways, then, I can see that I'm just like Haman. I can get 100 letters of thanks and praise about my writing, but I am easily disturbed by one criticism. Yes, I've got a little Haman ruling in my heart.

In this particular case, I knew that God had brought this criticism to me as a means of helping me see how weak I was and how I still needed His grace. As I prayed about the situation I decided that I would not defend myself. Instead, I would make room for God to defend me if He chose to do so. I decided that I would pray for the person who criticized me—pray that God would work in her life and bring her to Himself. I also realized I should look closely at her criticism because, even though it was obvious that the two of us were on completely different pages, I might learn something from her. And then finally, I decided to thank God for this opportunity to grow not only in my writing skills, but also in my character.

Perhaps God Sent the Critic

King David had a similar experience. His son Absalom had staged a coup, and David was fleeing from Jerusalem for his life. As David went along with his entourage, a man named Shimei started walking along beside him, cursing him. He said, "Get out, get out, you man of bloodshed, and worthless fellow!" (2 Samuel 16:7). I'm sure you can appreciate the way that these words must have stung David. There he was, fleeing for his life from his son, Absalom, and then Shimei piled on the criticism. Because he was the king, David could have ordered Shimei's immediate execution. In fact, one of his generals offered to do just that. But David's response was remarkable. He said, "If the Lord has told him to curse me, who am I to say no? My own son is trying to kill me, and this Benjaminite is merely cursing me. Let him alone, for no doubt the Lord has told him to do it" (2 Samuel 16:10-11 TLB).

Isn't that an amazing statement? David was able to look past the insults that were being hurled at him and see the Lord standing there behind them. He also had the hope that God would use this criticism for his good. "Perhaps," he said, "the Lord will see that I am being wronged and will bless me because of these curses" (2 Samuel 16:12 TLB). Later on, when David returned triumphantly from the battle, Shimei asked for forgiveness, and David granted it. David's heart of humility and trust in God was revealed by the way that he responded to criticism. David loved God's opinion, even when that opinion was one of discipline. He loved it more than he loved the praise of man.

How do you respond when you're criticized? What do you think of people who don't speak well of you? Who don't notice you? Who won't give you the time of day? Do you feel irritated or uncomfortable? Do you get angry, bitter, or resentful? Do you look for reasons to criticize in return, or do you try even harder to get their approval? Who do you *really* love? Do you see God standing behind them, drawing you to love and desire only Him?

Our Desire for Appreciation

As a counselor I frequently hear from wives who they believe they have a "need" to be appreciated by their husband. What they say to me usually goes something like this: "My husband doesn't appreciate anything that I do for him. Why, just yesterday I spent extra time making his favorite dinner, and I had the house and the kids nice and tidy when he got home. He just walked in, turned on the television, and plopped himself down in front of a T.V. tray and gobbled up his food. I don't think that he even noticed all that I had done for him. I'm tired of not getting the strokes that I need. In fact, I'm thinking that maybe I should leave him. After all, I have a need to be appreciated. My self-esteem is so low right now, I don't think I could stand another day with him."

A Right Perspective

Does this sound familiar? I imagine that it might because I know that there are times when I think the same sorts of things myself. Thankfully, God usually blasts me right out of this kind of thinking and I'm drawn to the truth. Here is a list of some of the ways that I fight against this kind of thinking:

- God has called me to be a servant, not a queen who is owed adoration or praise (Luke 22:26).
- I have been commanded to love and appreciate others, not to be loved or appreciated (John 13 and 15; 2 Corinthians 2:8).
- Since others have been commanded to love me, I must seek to make their task easy by serving and caring for them (Matthew 22:38-40).
- My desire for the praise of man is just that: a desire. It isn't a need. Everything that I truly need has been given to me in Christ (Luke 12:29-30; 2 Peter 1:2-4).

- I need to be focused more on being thankful for what the Lord and others have done for me (Psalm 28:7).

- I must seek to lay down my life in response to God's lovingkindness (Luke 9:23-24).

- The desire for praise is an avenue for sin that I must guard against (the book of Esther; Matthew 27:18).

- When I believe that I need praise, appreciation, or acceptance from others I become enslaved to their opinions. That slavery will hinder my ability to speak the truth in love to them (John 12:42-43).

The Praise of God

Have you ever thought about "the praise of God"? I'm sure that you've considered how you should praise God, but have you ever considered what God praises? Let's look at what the Bible has to say about this:

- *"Those who honor Me I will honor"* (1 Samuel 2:30).

During Israel's early history before the time of the kings, there was a priest named Eli. Eli had two sons who were ungodly and disobedient. Instead of disciplining them, as he should have, Eli pampered them. The Bible says that he honored his sons above God by letting them eat parts of the animal sacrifices that were forbidden. Eli didn't want to cross his sons or make them unhappy. Because of his lax discipline, God punished his household and said that if he had chosen to honor God, rather than his sons, God would have honored him.

I've often wondered if I honor my children—their favorable opinion, their happy faces—more than I honor God. Am I more interested in their friendship than God's? Am I afraid of their anger or displeasure? Do I consistently put God first in our relationship?

- *"If anyone serves Me, the Father will honor him"* (John 12:26).

Just like the fearful Jewish believers, we may be tempted to avoid serving Christ because we're seeking the honor that comes from others. For instance, I know that it's difficult for me to serve the Lord by witnessing to others. I've come to recognize that I don't want other people to think poorly of me, so I don't serve the Lord like I should in this area. My fear of what others might think overwhelms my desire for God's honor.

- *"Well done, good slave, because you have been faithful in a very little thing, you are to be in authority over ten cities"* (Luke 19:17).

In this verse from the parable of the fearful servant, I can see myself hiding my talent away when I'm fearful about how I'm going to be received—either by others or even by the Lord Himself. Am I willing to be faithful in even small tasks (that might seem big) or am I shirking back from the call that God has put on my life because I'm afraid that I might be criticized or might fail? Though at times it is difficult to do so, my heart's desire—and I hope yours, too—is to be faithful in the small tasks. To hear God say, "Well done, good servant" is the highest praise I could ever want in life—praise higher than any man could give.

- *"To those who by perseverence in doing good seek for glory and honor and immortality, [he will give] eternal life"* (Romans 2:7; see also 1 Peter 1:7-8).

What are you seeking? Are you with holy ambition seeking after the "glory and honor and immortality" that eventuates in eternal life? Or do you have other ambitions? Do you seek after the glory and honor that comes from being well liked, famous, or powerful? The challenge to us is to fix our hearts on one holy ambition and not to settle for the world's flimsy counterfeits. As the commentator Matthew Henry said, "Those that seek for glory and honor shall have them. Those that seek for the vain glory and honor of this world often miss them, and are disappointed...."[2] Os Guiness wrote that we are to live our whole lives before what he calls the "Audience of One." When we do so we can say to the world, "I have only one audience. Before you I have nothing to prove, nothing to gain, nothing to lose."[3] Living for an audience of one would simplify your life tremendously, wouldn't it? When God is your sole focus, decisions become so much easier. Your heart will know the peace and contentment that comes from seeking to please and glorify God alone. Your life will be richer because your pursuits will have eternal goals in mind, not earthly.

- *"...wait until the Lord comes who will both bring to light the things hidden in the darkness and disclose the motives of men's hearts; and then each man's praise will come to him from God"* (1 Corinthians 4:5).

No one can understand or judge the motives of our own hearts, let alone the motives of others. In this passage, Paul is cautioning his readers not to assume that they know or are able to judge the state of another person's heart. He goes on to say that God, who sees into all hearts and understands the thoughts behind the thoughts, will give praise to those who truly deserve it. I know that it is possible for me to do all the "right things" on the outside while my heart is far from God. In many ways I see that I'm like the Pharisees, whose outward conformity to religion was flawless but whose sole purpose was to garner the praise of man (Matthew 23:5). God is able to look deeply into my heart and assay the true quality of my work: Am I seeking after the praise of others, or am I seeking after the praise of Him alone? Do I fear what others might think of my actions and thus become indifferent to God's appraisal of my thoughts?

- *"It is not he who commends himself that is approved, but he whom the Lord commends"* (2 Corinthians 10:18).

I've noticed that in my own heart there is a desire to approve of myself. When I'm not able to do that (for whatever reason), sometimes I'll call my friends and try to get their approval. In the end, however, the truth is that it doesn't really matter if I or my friends commend me, or if I tell myself that I'm okay. The question is whether God commends me.

Of course, I know that if I hadn't received the righteousness of Jesus Christ, God would never approve of me. With Christ's record, though, I trust that God will commend me for Christ's sake. Paul, too, was anxious to obtain divine favor. He knew that God saw the true state of his heart, and it was because of God's grace that Paul could trust that the Lord would be pleased. Albert Barnes wrote that the goal of obtaining divine favor should be the "grand aim and purpose of our life; and we should repress all disposition for vain-glory or self-confidence; all reliance on our talents, attainments, or accomplishments...."[4] Is gaining *divine favor* the grand aim of my life? Or do I fear the disfavor of others, which in turn causes me to rely on my own "talents, attainments, or accomplishments" to quiet my fearful heart?

- *"He is a Jew who is one inwardly; and circumcision is that which is of the heart, by the Spirit, not by the letter; and his praise is not from men, but from God"* (Romans 2:29).

I'm sure that you're beginning to see there is a difference between the outward show that can result in the praise of man and the inner heart attitude that is pleasing to God. Are we strict about the behavior that others see yet self-indulgent when we are alone? Do we pursue the separation from the world that God sees and praises, or do we compromise and fudge on holiness so that people will like us?

Fear of Man vs. Fear of God

I frequently have the privilege of speaking on the topic of the fear of man or man-pleasing. On one particular occasion, my daughter was able to attend a conference with me. As I finished one part of my presentation, I encouraged all the women to get in groups and talk about the areas in their lives that needed growth. My daughter joined with one group of women and confessed to them that she really did struggle with wanting people to think well of her. After the meeting was dismissed she and I were talking, and she said, "I feel so badly that I confessed that to them. What must they think of me now?" We then looked at each other and started laughing. We could both see that we were still terribly tied to others' opinions. Even the confession of the sin of man-pleasing was hard because of our desire to have others think well of us.

The life of the apostle Peter is amazing in its display of the power of God's grace. Impetuous, boastful, brash, and cowardly, Peter is a wonderful example of God's ability to use sinful people and remake them into His image. We can all relate to Peter's denial of the Lord on the eve of the crucifixion. Our hearts break as we experience, with him, the soul-crushing look that passed between him and Jesus. In my own pride I think that if that had happened to me, I wouldn't be tied to the opinion of others. But Peter was, and the truth is that so am I.

Several years later, the apostles were working with the believers in Antioch, a Gentile city, when a number of Jewish Christian leaders came to visit. Peter, fearing what these men would think of him, started to eat with the Jews and ignore the Gentiles. Paul says that he opposed Peter for this action because it was hypocritical and he was leading others astray.

Why did Peter sin in this way? What was the door that led him to this hypocrisy? It was *the fear of man*. Peter was more concerned about what these leaders thought of him than about how his actions would affect those new Christians. Paul referred to the incident in the book of Galatians: "Am I now seeking the favor of men, or of God? Or am I striving to please men? If I were still trying to please men, I would not be a bond-servant of Christ" (Galatians 1:10).

The point that Paul is making is clear: When our lives are focused on gaining the favor of others or pleasing them for our own goals, we'll be at cross-purposes with the Lord. When it comes to this problem, there isn't much room for compromise: either we seek the Lord's favor and live accordingly, or we seek man's favor and live that way. Focusing on obtaining the praise of others and being fearful of criticism will always result in specific ways of living. *The way that we behave is always our method of obtaining what's important to us.* If it's the praise or approval of people that matters most to us, then we will always find ourselves in sinful behavior that reflects this.

The writer of Proverbs was aware of the great problems that come from living in this way. He wrote, "The fear of man brings a snare, but he who trusts in the Lord will be exalted" (Proverbs 29:25). In regard to the phrase "the fear of man brings a snare," think, if you will, about trapping an animal. You put out the bait, you set the trap, and you wait. Sooner or later, if the bait is interesting enough, your trap will be sprung. That's how it is with the fear of man. The word *snare* means "a trap, a hook, or a noose." Think of it in this way: The bait is something you love, a tasty treat called *others' good opinions.* Once you've developed a love for this dish, whenever you smell a compliment coming your way, or find yourself hungering for one, it's just a matter of time until you're entrapped by your own desire and find yourself sinning in some way, like Peter.

Freedom in Fearing God Alone

You'll find that knowing who you are and pursuing your God-given direction is liberating and joyous. In Woody Allen's film *Zelig* (1983), Allen portrays a man who is so desperate to be accepted by others that he becomes a human chameleon. The movie is an intriguing comment on the fears and insecurities that cause us to pander to others' opinions and lose our own soul. The only answer to this fear is the fear of God. This fear is the only one bright enough to act as the Polar Star in our lives. *What will best please and glorify Him?* is a question that should guide and focus our hearts. General Charles Gordon, a soldier who gave his life for England, once said, "Never pay attention to the favors or smiles of man; if [God] smiles on you, neither the smile or frown of men can affect you."[5]

The fear of man is a dangerous and terribly enslaving pitfall. As you seek to grow away from your fears, you'll begin to notice all the ways that you can become entrapped. Don't become discouraged! Although the fear of man is something that just about everyone struggles with, we know that the Lord can help us with it because He's the only one who ever completely conquered it. In fact, the Lord Jesus was never concerned about getting glory from others; John 5:41 says, "I do not receive glory from men." It was because He had the love of God and the desire to glorify Him within His heart that He was able to resist the temptation to seek to establish a worldly kingdom.

Applause from the Audience of One

Have you ever heard applause from just one person at the end of a performance? It's an embarrassing and eerie sound. But what if that one person is a king or ruler? That would make all the difference, wouldn't it? That's because the king's applause is more valuable than anyone else's. Think now about the words that your King has promised to speak to you: "Well done, good and faithful servant." Imagine the joy that will be yours when you hear them spoken, when you look into your Father's eyes and see His love. Picture what it will be like when you know that, *by His grace,* you've lived for Him. Won't every fight—all the wrestling with your fear—be worth it when you hear that one commendation? It won't matter if anyone else joins in the acclaim then, will it? You'll know the "eternal weight of glory far beyond all comparison" (2 Corinthians 4:17). Purpose to live for His applause now, and your name will be memorialized with all those who have heard, "Well done, good and faithful servant."

For Further Thought

1. In John 5:44 Jesus asks the question, "How can you believe, when you receive glory from one another and you do not seek the glory that is from the one and only God?" Meditate on this verse and ask the Lord to help you understand the connection between faith and seeking glory from man. Write your conclusions here.

2. As you consider whether you have a disposition to fear man or try to gain others' approval, can you identify behaviors that are linked to it?

3. Is there any person (or group of people) that you find yourself fearing? Spend some time praying for this person or these people, asking God to give you a Christlike love for them—a love that doesn't concern itself with how others respond to you.

4. The psalmist wrote, "The Lord is my strength and my shield; my heart trusts in Him, and I am helped; therefore my heart exults, and with my song I shall thank Him" (Psalm 28:7). Take time now to write a brief psalm of thanks to God for His goodness toward you.

5. Commit to memory Psalms 118:6 as you think about the way that you fear others: "The Lord is for me; I will not fear; what can man do to me?"

The Fear Caused
by Perfectionism

*"Therefore you are to be perfect,
as your heavenly Father is perfect."*

—MATTHEW 5:48

Martha was well respected and had many friends. She had all the qualities that people enjoy. She was conscientious, responsible, punctual, diligent, and unselfish. She never forgot a friend's birthday or missed an opportunity to send a thank-you note. She was dedicated and focused on her work for the Lord. Always neatly dressed, her home could be photographed at any time for *Home Beautiful* magazine. Yes, Martha had it all together. But Martha had a significant problem that was threatening to tear her whole life apart: Martha was a perfectionist.

When Martha came to me it was because she was struggling with anger and fear. Martha's children loved her but were afraid to cross her. Her husband knew that she had a problem with anger, but didn't understand why she couldn't just get over it. After all, Martha was so competent in other ways; why wasn't she able to overcome this problem?

Martha was beginning to suffer physically as a result of her perfectionism: She was unable to sleep; she awoke during the night worrying about tasks she had left undone. Sometimes her heart felt like it was going to burst because it was pounding so hard. At other times and for no apparent reason, she felt herself breaking out into a sweat and felt as though the room was closing in on her. It seemed that the more that she tried to control these distressing feelings, the stronger they became, until she felt as though she would lose her mind. She was tormented by all of the possibilities for failure that seemed so vivid in her imagination. She recognized that she was a perfectionist and supposed that her perfectionism was something she should try to overcome, but she was bewildered and confused. After all, hadn't God commanded her to be perfect?

More Righteous Than the Pharisees

In His famous teaching known as the Sermon on the Mount, Jesus made many astonishing statements. Among them is this one about His requirements for righteousness:

> I say to you that unless your righteousness surpasses that of the scribes and Pharisees, you will not enter the kingdom of heaven (Matthew 5:20).

To those who were listening to His words, this must have seemed like an impossible goal. More righteous than the scribes and Pharisees? How was that imaginable?

The people to whom Jesus was speaking were very familiar with the way that their religious leaders lived. They tithed mint and dill and cumin (Matthew 23:23); they fasted twice a week and paid tithes of all that they got (Luke 18:12). They lived lives that seemed, at least outwardly, to be impeccable. So for Jesus to tell His listeners that they needed to be *more* righteous than the scribes and Pharisees—people who were known for their strict adherence to a multitude of laws—was undoubtedly an intimidating command.[1]

Later on in Jesus' teaching on the Mount, He raised the bar even higher: "Therefore," He said, "you are to be perfect, as your heavenly Father is perfect" (Matthew 5:48). What? *More* perfect than even the Pharisees? As perfect as our heavenly

Father? These words *couldn't possibly* mean what they appear to mean! Or could they?

Perfection Like His

Anyone who really comprehends God's standard, as contained in His law and summarized in the Ten Commandments, has to admit that His perfection is simply beyond our grasp. In fact, the Bible even teaches that perfect law-keeping isn't possible by mere humans:

- Everyone has sinned and fallen short of the glory of God (Romans 3:23).
- There is no person on earth who is righteous and who continually does good and never sins (Ecclesiastes 7:20).
- The Scriptures insist that we are all prisoners of sin (Galatians 3:22).
- In God's sight no one is righteous (Psalm 143:2).
- No one can say that he hasn't sinned (1 John 1:8).

So, what did Jesus mean when He said that we had to be perfect? What would be the point of commanding us to be perfect if perfection is unattainable?[2]

Fleeing to Christ

It doesn't take long, if we're really serious about attaining God's perfection, for us to realize that we just don't make the grade. This is most easily seen in Jesus' summary of God's perfection and law. He taught that we must *love God with our whole heart, soul, mind, and strength and our neighbor the way that we love ourselves* (Matthew 22:37-39). These words are probably as familiar to you as they are to me. In fact, the problem isn't that we aren't familiar with them. The problem might be that we have heard them so many times they've lost their impact.

Love God with all of my being? Love my neighbor the way that I love myself?

The truth is that I do love God, but I'm sure that I don't always love Him with every fiber of my being. For instance, when someone gets in the way of my plans, I quickly forget that I'm to love him more than my plans. Instead, I usually proceed to do what I think I need to do in order to get what I want. And of course, when it comes to loving my neighbor the way that I already love myself, it's painfully obvious that I don't do that. When someone doesn't treat me the way that I want to be treated, I usually retaliate instead of being patient and gentle. Even the "righteous" Pharisees were filled with anger, envy, and hatred toward Christ, although they knew that God's law—which they claimed to obey—commanded that they were to love their neighbor the way that they loved themselves (Leviticus 19:18-19). So we have to face the fact that no one completely obeys even this most "simple" of all commands. As the Puritan Thomas Watson writes, "God is perfectly good. All the perfection we can arrive at in this life is sincerity."[3]

If it's true that I'm commanded to be perfect and yet I find that I am consistently unable to make the grade, what's the point of the command? It's as though God has commanded us to leap over the Grand Canyon. We may be willing to make feeble attempts, but the truth is that no matter how hard we try, or how many long-jump lessons we take, we'll always end up at the bottom, broken and in pieces. *And that's exactly the point.* The command to be perfect is given to us to drive us to the Perfect Law-Keeper: Jesus Christ. *Jesus flawlessly kept every point of God's law for us.* For those who recognize their utter helplessness, the offer of the righteous record of God's Son is just too good to pass up.

The first principle that we must learn about God's perfection is that it is available to us, but not because we're good enough to earn it. It is available only as we ask and believe in faith that Christ's perfect record could be applied to our life.[4] In the knowledge that His record is ours, we can find the peace and rest that we long for and the perfection that God demands. We don't have to ignore God's command; we can fulfill it. Because of the exchange that's taken place—my flawed record for Christ's perfect one—I can stand before the white-hot gaze of a completely holy God. And as far as He's concerned, I couldn't be more perfect. That's because I have *His* perfection.

Pressing On to Perfection

Is our desperate need for Christ's perfect record the only meaning to be found in His command to be perfect? Since as believers we now have His record applied to our lives, are we free to ignore God's command for perfection? No, we are also commanded to strive towards our own personal perfection and obedience.

- "Let us cleanse ourselves from all defilement of flesh and spirit, perfecting holiness in the fear of God" (2 Corinthians 7:1).
- "Aim for perfection…" (2 Corinthians 13:11 NIV).
- "Not that I have already obtained it or have already become perfect, but I press on so that I may lay hold of that for which also I was laid hold of by Christ Jesus" (Philippians 3:12).
- "We proclaim him, admonishing and teaching everyone with all wisdom, so that we may present everyone perfect in Christ" (Colossians 1:28 NIV).
- "…that you may stand perfect and fully assured in all the will of God" (Colossians 4:12).
- "…that you may be perfect and complete, lacking in nothing" (James 1:4).
- "…but like the Holy One who called you, be holy yourselves also in all your behavior; because it is written, 'You shall be holy, for I am holy'" (1 Peter 1:15-16).

It's verses like these that bring us to ask a very important question: If the purpose of Christ's command in Matthew 5:48 ("You are to be perfect, as your heavenly Father is perfect") is to help us recognize how desperately we fall short and cause us to see our need for Christ's righteousness, then why do all these verses emphasize our need to strive for perfection?

This is where our thinking might become fuzzy. That's because we tend to be confused about what the Bible refers to as "sanctification." *Sanctification* is that slow process of growth from our old ways of thinking and living to new, godly ones. Sanctification doesn't occur overnight—in fact, it's never fully completed until we reach heaven. At heart, it's the change that God is accomplishing through us: change into the image and character of His Son (Romans 8:29).

God has graciously given all true believers the perfect record of His Son. In addition, He placed our imperfect record on Christ and then executed His just wrath as Christ hung in our place on the cross. Because of this exchange, we can't be more righteous than He has made us. In the Bible, that's called *justification*. We've been made right by God.

Sanctification is also initiated by God's grace and is the process of changing our character from what it was when we first came to Him into what it should be: a reflection of His holiness. As you can see, there is a sense in which we are already perfect and there is another sense in which we are still striving towards it.

Christians who struggle with perfectionism need to recognize these distinctions. Because perfectionists set high standards for themselves (and others), they look at the commands to be holy or perfect and feel great condemnation because they don't measure up. They don't fool themselves about the need for perfection. In one of our talks about justification, Martha said to me, "Isn't God just kidding Himself?" She struggled desperately with her own feelings of inadequacy and God's demands. She needed to grow in her understanding of her justification, God's forgiveness, and her sanctification. She needed to see that she was already perfect in God's sight *and* that it was the work of the Holy Spirit that would enable her to grow daily in her personal perfection.

Whose Standards?

Martha, like many perfectionists, also struggled with setting up extrabiblical standards that she had to live by. For instance, a perfectionist might think that God's commands to be a good steward of her possessions means that she has to dust the house every day or wax the car every Saturday—without fail. A young girl might think that in order to avoid gluttony she should starve herself. An executive might believe that every document that is produced by his office has to be formatted in the exact way that he demands. For him, this would not be mere preference; rather, it would be the difference between right and wrong.

Elevating personal preferences to the status of moral rightness ultimately makes life oppressive. When Martha thought that her particular way of doing things was the only "right" way, she found that she was becoming increasingly angry and frustrated. In addition to this, she found herself filled with fear and panic. She became afraid when she saw that she couldn't obey all her standards perfectly. She panicked when others refused to live up to her expectations. She had the nagging feeling that everything was about to blow up because people just weren't doing things *properly*. She was also afraid to learn new skills because she was concerned that she might not do them perfectly. Perfection and the fear that stems from it had become a slave driver in her life that demanded more and more perfection to higher and higher standards.

If you find that you can relate to Martha, let me pose a few questions that might help you clarify your thinking. If you find that one or more of the questions resonate in your heart, then you'll want to look at the accompanying biblical truths and references that can help you as you look to God to change your heart.

- *Is this standard something that will really matter in eternity?*

Although keeping a neat home and running an efficient office are good goals, in the end it won't really matter if there is dust on your furniture when you stand before the Judgment Seat of Christ. God won't ask you, "Did you wash your car faithfully every Saturday?"

As you seek to sift through your standards to determine those that are eternally important and those that are self-imposed, ask yourself these questions: What is God Himself interested in? What will last throughout all time? What is eternal?

> ➤ God is holy and He's interested in your holiness. This holiness includes both your visible deeds *and* your motives (Psalm 11:4; Isaiah 6:1-7; 1 Corinthians 4:5; Hebrews 1:8-9).

> ➤ God's rulership and commandments are everlasting (Psalm 89; 93:2-5).

> ➤ God's kingly rule is founded upon His righteousness and justice. Our own personal standard of righteousness and our demands for justice are important only when they intersect with His (Psalm 97:2).

> ➤ Jesus Christ calls us to follow Him alone and to view all earthly situations and possessions as insignificant in comparison (Matthew 19:28-29).

> ➤ No one can stand before Christ because of his own good deeds. Only those who have been cleansed by His blood can pass God's test. Christ has promised forgiveness to all who ask

for it (Isaiah 45:21; Romans 3:26; 1 John 1:9; Revelation 5:7-10; 7:14-15).

➤ Only an awe-filled fear and worship of God will last, not our personal achievements or success (Revelation 19:4-5).

➤ Obedience to God's commands, rather than our own standards, is His measure (Revelation 20:12).

➤ We must humble ourselves and take His gracious gift rather than rely on our own goodness or ability to perform (Revelation 21:6-7).

Although measuring your standards by God's might seem intimidating at first, remember that God is on your side and He has promised to change your heart and life. As you put your trust in Him, letting go of some of the rules that seem to be so important, instead of chaos you'll find yourself freed from fears and enjoying great peace.

- *Are the standards or commands that I'm following easily discovered in Scripture, or am I adding to or twisting His commands? Would a casual reading of the New Testament affirm my standards, or are there other things more important to God?*

Although we are commanded to obey God in all of life, how we go about that is sometimes a matter of preference. For instance, as a woman I know that I am commanded to submit to my husband. If I decide that submission for me means that I never question my husband in public, that's fine. If I tell other women that they are obligated to obey my interpretation of God's command, then I am elevating my preference or personal conviction to the prominence that only God's Word deserves. I need to continue to remind myself that...

➤ The Pharisees, including Paul before his conversion, were known for their exact observance of strict rules, but they frequently elevated their own traditions to the status of a God-given command (Mark 7:1-13; Galatians 1:14).

➤ God's commands were summarized by Christ: "You shall love the Lord your God with all your heart, and with all your soul, and with all your mind" and "You shall love your neighbor as yourself" (Matthew 22:37,39). Our standards should be a reflection of the command to love.

➤ God's laws will help me grow in my ability to overcome self-indulgence. When I'm enslaved by impossibly high standards, I'll frequently find myself giving in to some form of self-indulgence. Following after my personal standards will only increase my pride (Colossians 2:21-23).

➤ The desire to add to God's commands doesn't flow from a love of God, but rather comes from the enemy (Genesis 3:1-19; 1 Timothy 4:1-3).

If, as you reevaluate your standards, you discover that they differ from the Lord's, or that you've made laws for yourself that don't coincide with His, you don't need to fear. Simply ask the Lord to show you His perfect law and to free you from your own. He'll do just that and you'll find that, as John says, "His commandments are not burdensome" (1 John 5:3).

• *Do I believe that I must obey this standard in order to please God?*

Martha thought that she was displeasing to God when she failed to dust her house every day. She thought that God wouldn't bless her efforts at mothering if she allowed her children to leave their beds unmade. Her own standards of cleanliness fostered despair, frustration, anger, and discouragement in her. Because she thought that God's pleasure with her mothering was based on her children's neatness, she ranted and raved whenever they left their clothes on the floor. Martha needed to renew her thoughts and remember that...

> ➤ God is pleased with His Son, therefore He was
> already pleased with her since she is "in Him"
> (Matthew 3:17; Ephesians 1; Philippians 3:9).

> ➤ She can grow more personally pleasing to Him
> as she seeks to obey Him out of love for His
> kindness and grace in her life (2 Corinthians
> 5:17; Ephesians 4:22-24; Colossians 1:10; Titus
> 3:4-7; Peter 1:5-9).

Are you "in Him"? If so, you can't be more pleasing to Him
than you already are. There isn't anything else you can do;
there is no perfection that can be attained that's better than
what you already have. Rest in the perfect life of Christ that
was lived for you and in the peace that comes from the knowledge of His pleasure!

- *Does this project or the way that I think it should be completed mean more to me than the people involved?*

Martha frequently found herself screaming at her children and
her husband because the house didn't look the way she thought
it should. She was filled with remorse about her treatment of her
children, but felt as though she couldn't help herself. She knew
that she should care more about them and the way that her
behavior was impacting them, but she feared that if she let go the
whole place would fall apart. When she came face to face with
these fears, Martha needed to remind herself that...

> ➤ In light of the command to love others the way
> that she loved herself, she needed to realize that
> people are always more important than projects,
> even projects initiated out of love for God (Luke
> 10:41-42).

> ➤ God rules sovereignly over the completion of all
> His will. It isn't her place to try to force Him or
> others to do what she thinks is necessary (Job
> 23:13; Psalm 33:9-11; 115:3; Isaiah 46:10-11;
> Acts 4:28; Ephesians 1:11).

Ask the Lord to open your eyes to the needs and struggles of those around you. He can cause your heart to overflow with love and fill you with the ceaseless joy that comes from laying down your life for others. You'll find this so much more satisfying than the fleeting pleasure you might get when you look at your perfectly clean house or a letter that is typed perfectly.

- *Do I feel guilty when I relax?*

Martha was exhausted. She never allowed herself time to relax because she always felt plagued by the little things that needed to be done. On one afternoon, when she could have rested or spent time with her children, she decided that she should make a blouse for her daughter. She felt pressured, frustrated, and angry while she worked, all the time blaming her husband for not making more money and her daughter for spoiling her other blouses. The truth was that she didn't have any joy in any task that she did because every job was done out of slavish obligation rather than love. Martha later sought to overcome this propensity by reminding herself that...

> ➤ God had given her the command to care for her body. Because of this command, she must be sure to get sufficient rest (Exodus 20:13; 1 Corinthians 3:16; 6:19).

> ➤ God has ordained the fellowship of other Christians to be a source of strength, growth, and renewal for her. She needed to schedule time just for fellowship (1 Thessalonians 4:18; 5:11; 2 Timothy 4:2; Hebrews 3:13; 10:24-25).

> ➤ God commanded the observance of a Sabbath rest in which she should give herself to God-centered ministry, prayer, meditation, and reading (Exodus 20:9-11; Leviticus 19:3; Isaiah 56).

Even Jesus took time away from the crowds for renewal. Learning to take time to relax isn't wrong; in fact, it's a necessity. God loves you and will help you accomplish everything you need to do for Him if you spend time in God-honoring rest.

- *Do I understand that all Christians, including me, are in a state of flux and growth? Do I give people room to fail, grow, and change? Am I patient with them?*

Martha didn't give herself or others room to grow or change. She demanded exact obedience from herself, her children, and her Christian leaders. She couldn't understand how people who said that they were Christians still struggled with sin the way that they did. She found herself becoming more and more impatient and intolerant with the failings of others, especially those in her own home. She needed to remember...

➤ Even the apostle Paul knew that he hadn't arrived at perfection (Philippians 3:12-13).

➤ Her sanctification is a process that is initiated and completed by God in His own time (Philippians 2:13).

➤ She should be patient with others who are struggling in the same way that she wanted them to be patient with her (Luke 6:31; Galatians 5:14; James 2:8-16).

➤ God is powerful enough to change anyone's character when it pleases Him to do so (Psalm 33:9-11; 115:3; Romans 8:29).

➤ Her failures and sins, as well as those of other people, are a powerful tool in God's hands to bring His children to Himself in humility and trust (Genesis 50:20; Exodus 4:21 and Romans 9:18-22; Matthew 26:69-75; John 13:38 and John 21:15-17).

Consider God's patience with you. It's really incredible, isn't it? He's been patient with me for so many years as I've struggled with my sin. I know that I need to be forbearing with others in the same way that He is patient with me. And when I am, God's peace will flood my heart, and I'll recognize that He's strong enough to change anyone—including me.

- *Do I tend to give up when I'm not perfect at my first (or second) attempt at something? Do I understand what it means to persevere even in the face of failure?*

Martha had been gifted with a beautiful voice for singing. Although she would use her gift when she was alone in her own home, she refused to use it at church. As we discussed this, she said that when she was a teen, on one occasion she had been asked to sing a solo and had forgotten the words to the song. She was humiliated and swore that she would never put herself in that position again. The Lord was working in Martha's heart to remind her of the truths that…

➤ God hadn't promised she would be perfect at everything she tried. Rather, He has promised to use everything in her life for good—that is, to change her character to become more and more like that of His Son (Deuteronomy 8:2-3,16; Zechariah 13:9; Romans 5:3-4; 8:28-29; 1 Corinthians 10:13; James 1:3-4; 1 Peter 1:7-8).

➤ God has promised to enable her to serve Him, and sometimes that means that her failure itself will serve His purposes (Psalm 76:10; Acts 4:27-28; 2 Corinthians 3:4-5; 4:7).

➤ God has promised that even though she continually failed and sinned, even though she was weak and frail, He is able to hold on to her and she will persevere to the end (John 6:39; 10:27-30; 17:12; 18:9; Colossians 3:3-4; 1 Peter 1:5).

Your confidence before God doesn't rest on your own perfections. In fact, it's *in spite* of your imperfection that you can stand confidently before God. He remembers your frailty and has great pity on you. "Just as a father has compassion on his children, so the Lord has compassion on those who fear Him. For He Himself knows our frame; He is mindful that we are but dust" (Psalm 103:13-14).

- *Do my priorities reflect a God-centered focus?*

As Martha saw the need to change some things in her life, she began to think soberly about her priorities. Although she was strongly committed to the Lord, she began to see that much of her life was taken up in "building her own kingdom." She saw that her undue focus on a clean house had more to do with her own pride than with her desire to build God's kingdom on earth. She began daily to pray, "Thy kingdom come, Thy will be done" in a way that reflected her new desire to put God first. She grew in this understanding as she continued to realize that...

> ➤ Jesus taught that the road to freedom from fear was found in seeking God's priorities—in seeking His kingdom and rule first (Matthew 6:25-33).

> ➤ Every activity and standard must be centered on the advance of God's kingdom rather than her own (Proverbs 3:9-10; Matthew 13:44-46; John 6:27).

It's as you focus your life on God's kingdom that He's promised to supply every one of your needs. Remember, He knows you and has pledged that "all these things will be added to you" (Matthew 6:33).

- *What is our ultimate goal in life? Are we seeking God's glory or our own?*

Martha's ultimate freedom from the enslaving demands of her perfectionism came as she embraced the supremacy of

God's glory in her life. Instead of focusing on what others would think of her, she began to focus on how to praise and exalt God in every circumstance. This was particularly difficult when her children failed to pick up after themselves, because she believed that their obedience would glorify Christ. Martha grew when she came to the understanding that her anger and demanding nature were more of a detriment to glorifying the Lord than her children's messiness. Yes, she was to train her children for the Lord, but she also needed to differentiate between her own standards and God's. She began to correct, nurture, and discipline her children for the Lord's glory, not her own. She matured as she recognized that...

> ➤ Every area of her life is to be focused on glorifying God (Psalm 115:1; Isaiah 43:21; Luke 20:25; 1 Corinthians 10:31; Ephesians 6:7; Colossians 3:17,23-24).

> ➤ Her own standards more accurately reflected her desire for personal aggrandizement rather than a genuine desire to draw others to Christ (Mark 9:38; 10:13; 15:10; Acts 19:13).

God has made the way for us to glorify Him and, as we do, we will find His joy flooding our soul more than we could ever have known trying to glorify ourselves.

• *Do I enjoy God or do I see Him as a demanding taskmaster?*

Martha had never really understood what was meant by the phrase "the joy of the Lord." She had heard it many times and although she did enjoy some times of laughter, she knew that when it came to joy, she was in the dark. She had never really looked at her relationship with God as being the source of true joy. Instead, she imagined God to be a demanding, gruff, angry, and powerful dictator. She falsely believed that she could never please Him and misinterpreted the command to deny herself to mean that she should live a gloomy, slavish existence. When her understanding of God's kindness and grace grew, her joy did also. Life became a pleasure and she looked forward to her times of prayer and worship as the delight of her day. She began to realize the truth of Puritan Richard Baxter's statement, "He will use you only in safe and honorable services, and to no worse end than your endless happiness."[5] And as Saint Augustine wrote, "God is man's happiness." Martha began to live as though He was her happiness. She knew that...

➤ Since God is the most winsome being in all the universe, her life should overflow with joy and gladness (1 Chronicles 16:27; Psalm 16:11; Acts 2:28; Ephesians 3:19; Jude 24; Revelation 7:15-17).

➤ In comparison to the joy of knowing Him, all the trials she had to face now—including her own and others' failures—are insignificant (Luke 6:22-23; Romans 2:7; 2 Corinthians 4:17; 1 Peter 1:7-8; 5:10).

Joy and happiness are your inheritance in Christ. Becoming free from man-made rules and laws and following Him with a thankful heart is the key to unlocking the pleasures that you've heard about. His joy is for you—not just everyone else—and it can be yours today.

Relaxed, Refreshed, and Rejoicing

As Martha grew in her knowledge of herself, God's perfect holiness and mercy, and His great plan to free her from her slavish fears, she found that the physical symptoms that she had experienced were diminishing. Whereas she once wakened during the night and would be tempted to fret about tasks she had left undone or problems that the family faced, she now spends those awake times focusing on God's goodness and love. She began to "anticipate the night watches" so that she could "meditate on [God's] word," as Psalm 119:148 says.[6]

Whenever she felt the familiar tightening in her chest she used it as a reminder to sit down and spend some time in conversation with her children or in prayer. She found that her home and life didn't fall apart like she had feared, but that, in fact, they were more peaceful. She developed a right perspective of Christ's perfect righteousness in her and the fact that we cannot be perfect yet should strive toward continued growth. As a result, her friends were more comfortable around her and enjoyed hearing about God's work in her life. Martha was well on her way to becoming a woman who reflected God's grace rather than her own self-focused goodness.

What's especially encouraging is that Martha isn't the only one who has experienced these changes. Others have, too, and you can as well. If after you've read this your heart longs for similar change, then why not take time now to pray that God will help you? This work begins with the confession that all your own goodness isn't good enough and that your focus has been in the wrong place. God is powerful and loving enough that He can change you in just the same ways as He changed Martha, and that work can begin right now. God is perfect and His standards are higher than you or I can ever attain; but, praise Him, He's made a way for you to hear Him say to you, "Well done, good and faithful servant."

For Further Thought

1. Review the questions that I've posed on pages 92-100. Which ones are particularly meaningful to you? Why?

2. Look up each reference listed by the questions you cited above. Write out the ones that speak specifically to your heart.

3. Have you identified any personal standards that do not fit the criteria given in this chapter? What are they?

4. How does devotion to these standards cause fear in your life?

5. What steps should you take to change them?

7
God Really Does Care for You

"...the best way to be comfortably provided for in this world, is to be most intent upon another..."[1]

—MATTHEW HENRY
Eighteenth-century author and theologian

$\mathcal{A}$s we traversed the back country of Chiapas, the southernmost state in Mexico, I was overcome by a sense of God's majestic care. Our little group intended to visit the proposed sight of a church. In order to get there we had to travel through little villages and over deserted mountain roads. As we crested a small hill, our eyes were greeted by the sight of many thousands of tiny purple flowers that completely blanketed a meadow. I looked around for huts or other signs of civilization and discovered, to my delight, that this meadow was attired by God for our pleasure alone. At that moment I remembered God's promise:

> Observe how the lilies of the field grow; they do not toil nor do they spin, yet I say to you that not even Solomon in all his glory clothed himself like one of these. But if God so clothes the grass of the field, which is alive today and tomorrow is thrown into the furnace, will He not much more clothe you?
> —Matthew 6:28-30

It is true. The most beautiful woman in the world, clothed with the most exquisite of attire, could never compare to the simple, astonishing beauty of that meadow. *If God is able to do this*, I thought, *isn't He also able to care for me?*

I'd like to tell you that I've always kept the thought of God's power before my eyes like I did that day. But the truth is that I sometimes have forgotten. I have worried. Sometimes I'm filled with unbelief and I wonder how God will ever work *this* mess out. Then the words of Jesus break through my doubts and I know: *If He can take care of that field and make it beautiful for His pleasure and share it with our little team, then He is certainly able to care for me in my trouble.* He melts my hard, unbelieving heart, and as my eyes fill with tears of thanks, my heart rests again in His Fatherly care.

Why Do You Worry?

The topic of worry is one that Jesus raised on several occasions. On one of those occasions He was seated upon the crest of a hill, speaking to His children as they sat all across the meadow before Him. Here's what He said:

> Do not be worried about your life, as to what you will eat or what you will drink; nor for your body, as to what you will put on. Is not life more than food, and the body more than clothing? Look at the birds of the air, that they do not sow, nor reap nor gather into barns, and yet your heavenly Father feeds them. Are you not worth much more than they? And who of you by being worried can add a single hour to his life? And why are you worried about clothing? Observe how the lilies of the field grow; they do not toil nor do they spin, yet I say to you that not even Solomon in all his glory clothed himself like one of these. But if God so clothes the grass of the field, which is alive today and tomorrow is thrown into the furnace, will

He not much more clothe you? You of little faith! Do
not worry then, saying, "What will we eat?" or "What
will we drink?" or "What will we wear for clothing?"
For the Gentiles eagerly seek all these things; for your
heavenly Father knows that you need all these things.
But seek first His kingdom and His righteousness, and
all these things will be added to you. So do not worry
about tomorrow; for tomorrow will care for itself.
Each day has enough trouble of its own.

—Matthew 6:25-33

I know that's a long passage, but if you just skimmed over
it, may I ask you to go back and reread it carefully? It's an
astounding discourse and one that will encourage and
empower you as you grow in your understanding of it.

Let's take some time now to delve into these precious words,
to really think about the implications of them. Our Lord was
seeking to free us from worry and fear, and since He knows us
perfectly, we would be wise to listen carefully and take heed to
His counsel.

Our Lord begins His instruction by commanding us to forsake worldly cares. He said, "Do not be worried about your
life, as to what you will eat or what you will drink; nor for
your body, as to what you will put on."

As soon as I read those words, I'm convicted that I ignore
them. I do worry about my life—how about you? I worry
about what's going to happen if the price of gasoline breaks
new heights, or what might happen if the economy goes into
a serious downward spiral. I worry about my children's health,
their spiritual life, their homes, their spouses, and their children and future. During 1999, I spent the whole year concerned about the Y2K bug. I have worried about my church,
my job, my counselees, my speaking opportunities, my
friends, my parents, my husband's parents, and on and on it
goes. If I were equipped with a "worryometer," I would probably discover I've been redlining for most of my adult life. And

then, of course, I worry about the fact that I worry so much while worrying about what might happen if I really gave it up. Sound familiar?

I'm convinced that when it comes to sins common to women, worry has to rank right up there. In fact, I've done some speaking on this topic around the country, and worry seems to be a hot-button for most of us. I'm not saying that men don't worry. My husband, Phil, who isn't usually entrapped by sinful worry, does fall into it sometimes. We can always tell when he's really distressed because a red line will appear on his forehead. I can tell by looking at his forehead (his worryometer) when he comes home from work what kind of day he's had. If he's "redlining" then I know that it's been a difficult day. I can see he's terribly concerned about something, and that now probably isn't the best time to complain that the faucet is still dripping.

Just Say *No*

In broaching the topic of worry, the Lord begins by saying, in essence, "Don't do it." When we're tempted to worry about something, we're supposed to say, "No." Worry is so common that we forget that it's actually a *sin*. Later, we'll look at why it is sinful, but for now we need to come face to face with the reality that it's just as sinful to worry as it is to disregard any other command from God. However, because worry is so common, and it appears (at least after a cursory glance) not to hurt anyone, we tend to give it a cozy little room in our hearts.

Matthew 6:25-33 isn't the only passage in the Bible that tells us not to worry. Consider the following:

- "Cast your burden upon the Lord" (Psalm 55:22).
- "Do not worry about how or what you are to say" (Matthew 10:19).
- "Be anxious for nothing" (Philippians 4:6).

- "...casting all your anxiety on Him, because He cares for you" (1 Peter 5:7).

Our Lord warns us against anxious thoughts that rob us of our peace. He cautions us against the speculations that spring from doubts and misgivings. Don't misunderstand: Jesus isn't talking about trying to turn off your brain. He isn't teaching, "Don't think at all about what you're going to eat, or wear, or your sleeping arrangements." No, what He's warning us about are those troubling, fearful thoughts that so effortlessly captivate our mind.

Our minds are incredibly powerful. One article states that it is "reasonable to conclude that the human brain has a raw computational power between 10^{13} and 10^{16} operations per second."[2] That's a staggering number, isn't it? (It's particularly hard for me to imagine that number is correct when I stare hour after hour at my computer screen, trying to figure out the right words to say as I write this chapter!) But the truth is that millions of thoughts can flash through our minds in a single moment—many times without our awareness. What's even more astonishing is that the God who created our brain's ability to function in this way has told us to control our thoughts!

In the parallel passage about worry in Philippians chapter 4, Paul does the same thing. He simply states, "Don't worry about anything." I know that if you are like me, it may seem that the command not to worry is similar to a command to make myself into a giraffe. There's just no way! No matter how many times I might try to stretch my neck out, my nature isn't that of a giraffe. And when it comes to worry, how could I possibly control my thoughts the way that I'm commanded? I admit that when I read the command not to worry, I sometimes feel like it's an impossible goal. Is it the same for you?

Once again we need to encourage ourselves, in the face of the seeming impossibility of this command, to flee to Christ. It is in Him, and *only in Him*, that you'll have the power you need to change. Jesus saw our inability to change when He told His followers,

> Abide in Me, and I in you. As the branch cannot bear fruit of itself unless it abides in the vine, *so neither can you unless you abide in Me.* I am the vine, you are the branches; he who abides in Me and I in him, he bears much fruit, *for apart from Me you can do nothing.*
> —John 15:4-5, emphasis added

Our loving Lord is saying to us, "You can't do this on your own. You can't change your thinking so that it will produce good fruit unless you're getting your strength from Me." The apostle Paul, who had one of the greatest minds of all time, recognized his inability to change. He knew that he had to utterly rely on the Lord. That's why he said, "I can do all things *through Him who strengthens me*" (Philippians 4:13, emphasis added).[3]

Overcoming our propensity to worry is not something that we can do without Christ's help. The good news is that He's available, ready to help us when we ask. We can pray along these lines:

> *Father, I thank You that Your ears are always open to my thoughts and my words. I ask that You would forgive me for worrying and that You would enable me, in Your time, to triumph over my worry. I praise You that You've promised to strengthen me and cause me to be fruitful in my life.*

The Focus of Our Worries

Let's go back to Matthew 6 and examine what the Lord identified as the focus of our anxious thoughts. He said, "Do not be worried about your life, as to what you will eat or what you will drink; nor for your body, as to what you will put on" (verse 25). As I look over that list it's easy for me to think, *Hey, I don't worry much about what's for lunch or what I'm going to wear. I guess I'm really okay.* But then I think more deeply about the implications of the Lord's words. Do I worry about my *life*? Do I worry about my *body*? Yes, I must admit that I do. I worry about every facet of my life: my future, my past, what's going to happen today. The word "life" includes everything that I am. I worry about whether I'll have the resources I need in order to do what I need to do. I worry about my health and the effects of my worry on my health. I worry about my children's health, my grandchildren's health, my parents' health, my boss's health.

Listen now to how our Lord responds to our worries:

• *Life consists of more than these outward concerns.*

Your life isn't upheld through the gratification of your temporary desires: What will I wear, what will I eat or drink, where will I live? Your body may benefit from having warm clothing, healthy food, and secure shelter, but the source of your existence doesn't ultimately come from these things, but from the God who is actively sustaining you. God, who is daily preserving your life (a task much more difficult than merely providing food), is able to supply the means that are necessary for your continued existence. The Lord invites you to put your complete trust in Him. Shall He who created your body be unable to protect, sustain, and provide for your every need?

• *God cares perfectly for lesser creatures like birds and flowers, and it should be obvious that He can care for you.*

A dear friend gave me a lovely book entitled *The Art of God.*[4] Filled with stunningly beautiful pictures of God's creation, every time I look at the book I'm amazed as I observe our world's wondrous beauty, symmetry, diversity, and order. It is the Lord Himself who causes the earth to rotate around the sun, who brings about the seasons, who causes rain to fall on the earth. It is as Paul wrote:

> Christ himself is the Creator who made everything in heaven and earth, the things we can see and the things we can't...all were made by Christ for his own use and glory. He was before all else began and it is *his power that holds everything together.*
> —Colossians 1:16-17 TLB, emphasis added

But God isn't interested in just the big things, like holding our universe together. He's also wholly involved in the little details: the food and life of seemingly insignificant little birds; the beauty of flowers that appear for only a day or two; yes, even the number of hairs on our head (Matthew 10:30). God isn't merely overseeing our world from afar, only managing major concerns. No, He's right here, next to us, overseeing and ordering every little detail of our lives. God is here and He's involved. And if He's powerful enough to beautifully clothe the grassy meadow and caring enough to provide little seeds for a sparrow, then He certainly should be able to take care of us.

• *Worry doesn't have the capacity to change anything.*

Pragmatism is a philosophy that evaluates truth claims by whether or not they "work." Jesus said, "Who of you by being worried can add a single hour to his life?" (Matthew 6:27). What was He trying to teach us? *Our worry doesn't accomplish anything.* So even if we're just going to look at our worry pragmatically, Jesus assures us that it's a useless exercise. It can't change anything. It won't make you live one moment longer than God has ordained. It won't influence whatever you might face in the future. *Worry is powerless.* All of the hours that I have spent worrying and fretting over my problems, whether imagined or real, have been *a waste of time.* Of course, the sad reality is that I could have used that time more profitably in real problem solving.

• *Your worry is a road sign pointing to a deeper problem: unbelief.*

Jesus really got down to brass tacks when He said, "If God so clothes the grass of the field, which is alive today and tomorrow is thrown into the furnace, will He not much more clothe you? *You of little faith!*" (Matthew 6:30, emphasis added). Little faith! Think about those words. The Lord equates our worry with a lack of faith.

Why does the Lord say that worry is unbelief? How does my worry reflect the level of my faith? My worryometer is also a faithometer; and in this case it isn't my faith that's red-lining—it's my unbelief. Why is worry unbelief? Because it has its roots in doubt about God's character. It questions His Fatherly care and provision. When I worry about what's going to happen to my life, what I'm really saying is, "God, You can't handle this. You're either too weak, uninterested, unloving, or not smart enough to take care of my life. I've got to devote all my attention to sorting this situation out on my own."

God has directed His children not to worry; He's classified worry as sin. Why? Because worry flows out of a distorted or incomplete view of His nature and character. God has revealed Himself both in His creation and in His Word. We are obligated by this self-revelation to know Him as He is. Although we'll never completely understand Him or be able to fully comprehend His nature, He's given us everything we need to know about what we need to know. When we spend our days worrying, we're disregarding what He's told us about His perfect holiness, power, wisdom, and love. We're saying, "I have to handle this because You can't be trusted."

Worrying is also sinful because it elevates our thoughts and abilities to a godlike position. When we worry we're putting our trust in our thoughts and in our ability to "work things out" in our mind. It is because of this that worry is linked together with pride in 1 Peter 5:5-7:

> ...all of you, clothe yourselves with humility...for God is opposed to the proud, but gives grace to the humble. Therefore humble yourselves under the mighty hand of God, that He may exalt you at the proper time, casting all your anxiety on Him, because He cares for you.

When we worry, we're proudly trusting in our own strength and power. We're opposing God, who has said to put our trust in Him and to humble our hearts under the mighty hand of His providence. We're depending on ourselves instead. We are exalting ourselves as being mightier than Him. We're impatiently waiting for Him to do what we think He should—and when He doesn't, we think that we have to figure out how to take care of the matter.

- *When we worry we're acting like orphans; we're forgetting that God is our Father.*

The Lord brought this point home when He taught,

> Do not worry then, saying, "What will we eat?" or "What will we drink?" or "What will we wear for clothing?" For the Gentiles eagerly seek all these things; for your heavenly Father knows that you need all these things.   —Matthew 6:31-32

I grew up in a home without a father. My mother worked hard all of her life to provide for my brother and me, but I never really experienced the security that having a father would have given me. In some ways I'm glad for that, because I've been taught not to put my trust in a mere earthly father, but in my heavenly one.[5] I've had to learn *from Scripture* what the Lord says about His Fatherly care, and I'm thankful for that.

When we worry and fret about our perceived needs, we're forgetting that we have a Father who knows what we really need even before we ask. Of course, there is usually a great difference between what *I* think I need and *God's* perspective. I must humble myself then, conceding to His wisdom, and believe that He knows what's best for me and that He will give me everything that's truly necessary for me. Paul tells us in Romans 8: "If God is for us, who is against us? He who did not spare His own Son, but delivered Him over for us all, *how will He not also with Him freely give us all things?*" (Romans 8:31-32, emphasis added).

The Father who gave me the most needful and precious gift of all, His Son, will not fail to provide everything I need. Those who don't know God's care have to spend their time worrying about how they're going to survive; they don't have a choice. But we who have known God and have experienced His love ought to be beyond worry, shouldn't we? Do we believe that God is wise enough to know what we need and powerful enough to give it to us? What need then do we have of worry?

• *Worry proves that I'm headed in the wrong direction.*

Rather than spending my days pursuing my own desires and worrying about my future, I need to be actively focusing my energies on God's kingdom and His righteousness. Jesus said, "Seek first His kingdom and His righteousness, and all these things will be added to you" (Matthew 6:33).

The primary focus of our life is to be on establishing His kingdom and growing in His righteousness. Matthew Henry said that we are to "mind heaven as our end and holiness as our way."[6] We are to make the desire to know Him, please Him, and delight in Him the dominant end of all we do.

Martha, the sister of Lazarus and Mary, was a woman filled with worry. The Lord had come to her home, and while she was busy preparing a meal, her sister, Mary, sought the kingdom of God. Here's how Luke records the event:

> Martha was distracted with all her preparations; and she came up to Him and said, "Lord, do You not care that my sister has left me to do all the serving alone? Then tell her to help me." But the Lord answered and said to her, "Martha, Martha, you are worried and bothered about so many things; but only one thing is necessary, for Mary has chosen the good part, which shall not be taken away from her."
> —Luke 10:40-42

What was that one necessary thing that Mary found and Martha missed on this occasion? It was the kingdom of God. It was growing in righteousness. Martha's worry had distorted her perspectives. Instead of recognizing that Jesus was on His way to die for her sins, she questioned Jesus' care for her. Instead of growing in holiness, she was angry and envious of her sister. She missed the primary purpose of the day and worried instead about making lunch.

Do you see yourself in Martha? I know that I do. I'm so busy trying to do things for God (as if He needs me!) that I miss what's really important. I need to grow in my own desire to please, bless, and glorify Him. I need to grow in holiness and in my understanding of His nature. These things take time, but they are what I must focus my energies on.

But, you might be thinking, *what would happen about lunch if I didn't worry about it?* Jesus reminds us that God knows what we need and that everything that is necessary will be provided by Him. Think of it: Martha was worried about putting lunch together for the One who made lunch for 5,000 people from almost nothing! If He was hungry, He could have multiplied loaves or had the birds bring them food. "He who giveth you the golden treasures of heaven will not allow you to want for the copper treasures of earth."[7] Do you trust that God is able to provide for you?[8]

I'm not saying that you shouldn't be concerned about your responsibilities. What I am saying is that there is a difference between trying to be responsible, as an act of joyful worship, and worrying about the outcome of your labors. Jesus kept busy fulfilling all the work the Father had for Him, but He never "freaked out" about getting things done. That's the difference between working in faith with cheerful zeal and working in your own efforts in slavish drudgery.

• *You can't do anything about what might happen tomorrow.*

In a very succinct way, Jesus completes His discourse on worry with the following words: "Do not worry about tomorrow; for tomorrow will care for itself. Each day has enough trouble of its own" (Matthew 6:34). You and I have only one day in which to handle our problems: today. We can't handle the troubles of tomorrow because tomorrow isn't here yet. Worry saps our strength for today's battles by getting us to focus on tomorrow's. Although it isn't wrong to make plans for our future, we must always do so with God's rule in mind (James 4:13). Worry tends to distract us; it draws our thoughts down little paths of imagined possibilities. It keeps us from focusing on the opportunities that are right before us, and draws us away.

Overcoming Your Worry

The apostle Paul laid out three practical steps for overcoming worry. He said,

> Don't worry about anything; instead, *pray about everything;* tell God your needs and don't forget to *thank him for his answers.* If you do this you will experience

God's peace, which is far more wonderful than the human mind can understand. His peace will keep your thoughts and your hearts quiet and at rest as you trust in Christ Jesus....*Fix your thoughts on what is true and good and right.* Think about things that are pure and lovely, and dwell on the fine, good things in others. Think about all you can praise God for and be glad about. Keep putting into *practice all you learned from me* and saw me doing, and the God of peace will be with you.

—Philippians 4:6-9 TLB, emphasis added

Do you see Paul's steps for overcoming worry? The first is to *pray with thanksgiving* about all your concerns. When God commands you not to worry He isn't telling you to pretend you don't have any problems. No, He's telling you to focus all your energies on thankful prayer. That way, when a troubling thought shoots into your mind you can say: "I'm not going to think about this anymore; I've already prayed about it."

The next step to take is to learn, by God's grace, to control your thoughts. Paul tells us that there are eight filters through which we should judge our thoughts. You'll find them in the chart below:

Thought Filters:	Ask Yourself:
True	Is what I'm thinking *true* about God, particularly His fatherly care for me?
Honorable	Do my thoughts honor God? Do they reflect the knowledge that He is wonderful, kind, loving, wise, and powerful?
Right	Are my thoughts holy, righteous, or just? Are they the kind that the Lord Himself would think?

Pure	Do my thoughts cast doubt on God's goodness or the truth of His promises? Do they elevate my own importance or desire?
Lovely	Do my thoughts flow from a heart filled with tenderness and affection for the Lord? Would my thoughts bring Him pleasure?
Of Good Repute	Are my thoughts of good repute? Are they grounded in faith?
Excellent	Do my thoughts cause me to be fearful, or do they fill my heart with courage and strong commitment to virtuous living?
Praiseworthy	Would the Lord commend my thoughts? Would they bring Him glory?

Finally, Paul tells us that we need to *practice* the disciplines of thankful prayer and daily evaluation of our thoughts. For me, this is where the rubber meets the road. I tend to be a pretty good beginner, but not such a great "practicer." Practice means that I won't get it right the first (or even the second) time I try. I'll have to work hard to control my anxious thoughts, but I can rest in the knowledge that God is working with me in this.

Paul encourages us to work at this by giving us a precious promise. He writes, "The peace of God, which surpasses all comprehension, will guard your hearts and your minds in Christ Jesus," and "the God of peace will be with you" (Philippians 4:7,9). What would you do to find the peace of God and know that the God of peace was with you?

Peace Can Be Yours...Today

As we close this chapter on worry, I want you to remember that God's peace is available to you today. The peace that He's promising you is not protection from trials or storms. No, it's the peace that you can find in the midst of any storm. It's the peace that will protect your heart from turmoil when you focus on His kingdom and righteousness—when you pray with thanksgiving and learn, by His grace, to filter your thoughts.

The peace that He has for you is beyond your understanding. It's better than you can possibly imagine, and it will guard you from falling into those dark depths of despair that worry and anxiety can dig in your heart. "Peace, be still," the Lord says to your agitated heart. "I'm the God who holds today and all your tomorrows. You can trust in My Fatherly care."

For Further Thought

1. Make a list of your worries. Put a check mark (✓) next to those that aren't in your power or your responsibility to do anything about. These are the concerns that you'll need to pray about and *leave* in the hands of God. Put an arrow (←) by those that you have responsibility for and make another list (in order of importance) of these tasks that you need to complete. Pray about these as well.

My Worries	✓ or ←	My Responsibilities
		1.
		2.
		3.
		4.

		5.
		6.
		7.
		8.

2. Make a "Thank List." List the ten things you are most thankful for. Your list might include God's benefits to you (such as salvation or His Word or grace) along with your earthly blessings (family, friends, provisions). Just as you spent time in prayer about the concerns you listed above, spend some time thanking God for everything on your list. This will help you to have faith that God really is in control and will help to focus your thoughts on His kindness rather than on what you think you still need.

3. During the day, when distressing thoughts intrude into your mind, remind yourself that you have already prayed about your concerns and review the items on your Thank List. As you do so, God's peace will flood your heart and guard you from fear and further distress.

4. When you begin to feel as though you're getting anxious, stop to evaluate your thoughts using the filter on pages 118-119. I've included this filter in Appendix B so that you can make copies and keep them with you.

The Security
of God's Sovereignty

*"Deny that God is governing matter, deny that He is
'upholding all things by the word of His power,'
and all sense of security is gone!"*[1]

—ARTHUR W. PINK
Bible teacher, theologian, and author

*W*hen Carol came to me, it was with a sadness that was threatening to overwhelm her soul. Carol's church, where she had been fed and blessed for a number of years, seemed to be coming apart at the seams. Her pastor had been caught in sin, her friends were leaving, and her family was in turmoil. It seemed as though a day didn't go by without another bit of discouraging news surfacing. The apparent eventual demise of her church was the topic of every conversation and the fount from which numberless tears had flowed in prayer. People were discouraged; friendships were being torn apart; a wonderful pastor's ministry was in disgrace.

Carol found herself waking up at night, filled with fear. She feared the effect that these problems would have on her family. She dreaded having to search for a new church. She feared that God was punishing her, that somehow the problems were her fault, that the world was spinning out of control. Where was God in all this? Did He even care?

Barbara's life seemed to be made up of one crisis after another. For years she had faced tragedy after tragedy. One baby had died at childbirth. Her daughter had been crippled in a serious accident. Her husband felt that he couldn't stand the pressure and left her for another woman. And now Barbara's mother had cancer. Although she'd believed in God her whole life, she was beginning to wonder if perhaps she had believed in vain. If there was a God, was He really in control? Or did He just sit impotently in heaven, wringing His hands over all the troubles on earth?

On the way home from the doctor's office, Dave's head was spinning. What had the doctor said? *Leukemia?* What was that? How could his wife Anne, a woman so young, so beautiful, have a disease that sounded so frightening? Sure Anne had felt tired. What mother of four wouldn't? But *leukemia?* What did this mean? Where was the God that they had trusted? What would life hold for them now? Would he have to raise their children on his own? How could he face life without her? Had God made a mistake? Was He watching?

Nate's little delivery business was finally growing. After years of advertising, driving routes over and over again, working hours on end, Nate was beginning to feel that he was finally getting ahead. He had a steadily growing clientele and a number of leads for more customers. He had six trusted employees who drove through the streets of his town. Everything seemed to be coming together. Then, Mac, one of his employees, after drinking on the job, crashed his delivery van into a family car and seriously injured a little three-year-old girl. Nate had to face the likelihood that he was going to lose his business, his vans, and even his home. Everything that he had worked so hard for had vanished because of one stupid mistake. He was tormented by thoughts of his responsibility for the accident: Had he not been watchful enough? Why hadn't God opened Nate's eyes to Mac's drinking problem? Why would God let Nate spend all those years building a business if it was going to end like this? Had he missed God's will? Was God really in control?

Jan had no one to blame but herself. She was the one who had disobeyed her parents. She was the one who had run away and lived a wild life on the street. Even though she had become a Christian and was living with a godly family, she was the one who had tested positive for HIV. She believed that God had forgiven her sins, but now, just when it seemed that He should have been pleased with her, she was facing her own death. Maybe God hadn't forgiven her...maybe He really wasn't in charge...maybe she shouldn't trust Him. Jan was beginning to think that perhaps she should just throw in the towel. If God couldn't keep her from this terrible sickness, why should she serve Him?

Theology—Does It Really Matter?

In recent years, there has been a general consensus that theology—or a systematic study of God—is not really relevant or important. Nowadays, some people even think that it isn't necessary to have fixed beliefs about God or the Bible. For instance, some people feel that what one believes isn't really important just so long as there is *some sort of belief* in *some sort of god*. Theology? Doctrine? Christians don't really need all that high-sounding rigmarole, do they? After all, theology just separates people and causes fights. Shouldn't we all work at loving one another and leave all that quibbling to the Bible scholars in their ivory towers?

Although it might not seem apparent at first glance, every one of the stories that I opened this chapter with presents a *theological problem*. That's because theology is simply *a system of beliefs about God*. Everyone has a theological perspective; everyone has a belief system. In fact, you don't have to be trained in theology to be a theologian. Everybody is a theologian of some sort. Even an atheist has a theological perspective: His theology tells him that God doesn't exist. The question is not whether you have a set of beliefs about God that govern your view of life, but whether those beliefs are based on truth. One question you can ask yourself is this: Will my beliefs stand the test of real life before the real God? Do your beliefs calm your fears, soothe your conscience, direct and motivate you in the face of the kinds of troubles we just read about? It's usually not until we face an insurmountable difficulty that we realize that our house might be built on something less than the reinforced concrete of biblical truth.

Crucial Questions with Consoling Answers

In this chapter, we're going to ask two theological questions. First, Is God sovereign? The word *sovereign* simply means that God is absolutely free to do whatever He wants. As Jerry Bridges writes,

> He does whatever pleases Him and determines whether we can do what we have planned....No creature, person, or empire can either thwart His will or act outside of the bounds of His will.[2]

Of course, God's ability to do exactly what He wants must be understood in the context of His character. For instance, since God is completely holy, it is not possible for Him to sin. God is able to do whatever He has decided to do, and everything He has decided to do is always perfectly holy, perfectly just, perfectly loving, and perfectly wise. It is His character and power that makes Him God. If His character and power are anything less than this, He is no longer God.

The second question is this: If God is sovereign, how can that help us overcome our fears? When we're facing the difficulties of life—when we're filled with fears and anxiety and when we're feeling as though our lives are coming apart at the seams—it is the truth that God is sovereign that will bring us hope, peace, and confidence. It's the truth that He's perfectly holy, perfectly just, perfectly loving, and perfectly wise coupled together with His perfect power that will be our mainstay during times of trial.

If you're not comfortable with the thought of reading a whole chapter about theology, let me encourage you to read on. This will not be a dry discussion about facts that don't really matter much. Rather, I hope you'll begin to see that the doctrine of the sovereignty of God can be one of the most comforting and enlivening truths you could ever know. It's the knowledge that God is in control that will calm your greatest fears and cheer you during your most difficult trials. It's this knowledge that Carol, Barbara, Dave, Nate, Jan, and you and I need. So, let's take a closer look at who God says He is, and then we'll look at how these truths can help us with our fear and worry.

What God Says About Himself

The most direct way for me to get to know you would be to ask you questions and then listen to your answers. Likewise, the most direct way we can get to know God is to look in the Bible. God's own testimony about Himself is reliable because He's completely acquainted with His own nature. And because God's self-knowledge is without error, we can trust that He hasn't deceived or confused us about His power or purpose. So let's look briefly now at what God says about His own sovereignty:

- God says that He controls *every event* for His own honor and glory: 1 Chronicles 29:10-11; Psalm 103:19; Proverbs 16:33.

- He determines the seasons, the weather, the growth of crops: Genesis 8:22; 1 Kings 8:35; 2 Chronicles 7:13-14; Amos 4:7; Isaiah 5:6; Haggai 1:10-11.

- God determines the length of our lives: Job 14:5; Psalm 68:20; Acts 17:26.

- God is completely free to do whatever He wants, including overruling our decisions: Job 23:13; 42:2; Psalm 33:9-11; 115:3; Proverbs 19:21; 21:30; Isaiah 43:13.

- God doesn't need anything from us to enable Him to rule sovereignly: Acts 17:24-25.

- It's God who gives us success: John 15:5; 1 Corinthians 3:7; 2 Corinthians 12:9.

- God brings to Himself those whom He predestines to come to Him: Matthew 11:27; John 1:13; 6:65; 12:39-40; Romans 9:15; Ephesians 1:11; Philippians 2:13.

- God gives gifts and callings according to His sovereign will: 1 Corinthians 12:11; Ephesians 4:11; Hebrews 2:4.

- God is sovereign over everything, even our sin, rebellion, and foolishness: Genesis 20:6; 50:20; Exodus 4:21 and Romans 9:18; 1 Kings 12:15; Acts 2:23; 3:18; 5:38-39.[3]

I know that I've given you a lot of references. That's because they are important for us to know. The greater our awareness of God's sovereignty, the more of an impact this fact will have on our lives. This, in turn, will help us to become free of our worries and fears. I want you to know that the Bible is crystal-clear about God's sovereignty and that you can fully rely on Him and what He's said about Himself.

Why God's Sovereignty Is Important for You

You might be wondering why I would take time to talk about God's sovereignty in a book about fear and worry. For this very reason: *God's sovereignty is the only safe harbor when we're assailed by the winds of fear, doubt, and worry.* Bible teacher

Arthur Pink wrote, "Deny that God is governing matter, deny that He is 'upholding all things by the word of His power,' and all sense of security is gone!"[4] If tragedies, illnesses, and even our sinful choices are just an accident or random circumstance, then how will we ever find any solace or comfort? If there is one tiny molecule floating around the universe that isn't under God's direct control, we'll never find the peace and joy that He's promised. We won't find it because we'll always be wondering whether we're out of God's will or in a problem that's taken Him by surprise or that He's incapable of handling.

Before He was crucified, Jesus spent a lot of time talking with His disciples, preparing them for the difficulties they would soon face. He warned them about the upcoming trials; He talked of His Father's plan and power. He wanted them to know that He was in control even though it would seem to them that their world was falling apart. He said,

> Behold, an hour is coming, and has already come, for you to be scattered, each to his own home, and to leave Me alone; and yet I am not alone, because the Father is with Me. These things I have spoken to you, so that in Me you may have peace. In the world you have tribulation, but take courage; I have overcome the world.
>
> —John 16:32-33

What was Jesus telling the disciples? He was saying that He was about to be taken from them—and more significantly, that they were going to desert Him! They were about to scatter from Him like frightened little sheep. They were going to abandon Him. What would cause His faithful followers, men who had left behind all their worldly possessions to be with Him, to run? Fear. They were about to come face to face with one of their greatest fears: the death of their beloved Leader and the possibility that the last three years of their lives had been spent in vain.

Jesus wanted the disciples to know that He already knew of their coming panic and had planned for it. He wanted them to know that His Father, the sovereign Lord, wasn't going to forsake them. He wanted them to have peace, even at the time of their greatest failure and fear. Now, notice that He didn't promise they wouldn't have problems. In fact, He had promised them just the opposite: He had promised them that their lives would be filled with "tribulation." They would experience great anguish and trouble. Why? Because His Father was too weak to stop it from happening? No, they would experience troubles because it was God's will for them. He wanted them to know that His Father really was in control. God was in control of Judas, He was in control of the Pharisees, He was in control of the weak Roman governor Pilate. That's what Acts 4:27-28 says:

> For truly in this city there were gathered together against Your holy servant Jesus, whom You anointed, both Herod and Pontius Pilate, along with the Gentiles and the peoples of Israel, *to do whatever Your hand and Your purpose predestined to occur* (emphasis added).

Between the crucifixion and resurrection, the disciples would have found it tough to believe that God was in control of Judas' treachery, the cruel injustice of the Pharisees, and the disappointing weakness of Pilate. Not until they made it through the trial, after the resurrection, could they see God's hand. But before? They were blind to it. Even though Jesus warned them and told them that His Father was with Him, they still fled in fear. They didn't really understand that God was in control, did they?

Peace in the Midst of Chaos

Why did Jesus warn the disciples? What did He say His goal was? His goal was *for them to have peace*. And where would that peace come from? It would come from the knowledge that He had *overcome the world*. The world included Judas, Pilate, and the chief priests who had brought Jesus to trial. Even though it seemed as though they were calling the shots, they weren't really the ones in charge. They weren't going to overcome God or His plan. No, Jesus said, "Take courage; I have overcome the world." He wanted them to know His peace, so He told them that He was in control. Jesus had already subdued the world and everything in it to Himself. He had already conquered!

Do you see how God's sovereign control of the world is the key to your peace? When it seems as though everything you hold dear is being torn away—when it appears that there is no rhyme or reason to the events that are bombarding you—do you see how the knowledge of His power can calm your soul? When it appeared that wicked men could bring an end to God's plan, Jesus wanted His followers to know that He was still in control. They could have peace because the One who said, "Be still" to the storm and calmed the seas was still in control.

A God You Can Trust

Knowing that God is in control isn't much of a comfort if you don't know what His character is like. He might be a sovereign despot, ruling the universe with hatred and malice. Or He might be a powerful but bumbling old fool who doesn't really know what's best for us. Or He might be a vengeful magistrate, like Javert, the malicious policeman in *Les Miserables* who pursued Jean Valjean to the ends of the earth in the name of the law. If you don't know the nature of the God who wields all this power, the knowledge that He is sovereign probably won't bring you peace. In fact, it might make you even more fearful. Here's a brief overview of what the Bible says about God's character:

- *God is perfectly wise.* That means that He always knows what is best (Romans 16:27).

- *God is completely holy.* His holiness controls all His actions so that He never acts in any way that is unholy, unwise, or unloving (Isaiah 6:3; Revelation 4:8).

- *God is utterly loving.* His love always constrains and guides Him to give us what we truly need (1 John 4:8,16).

- *God is infinitely merciful.* His mercy flows out to all of His creation at all times in that He never gives any of us what we really deserve (Exodus 34:6-7).

God is not a malicious despot, a bumbling old fool, nor a celestial policeman. No, He's completely wise, holy, loving, and merciful. When He acts in His sovereign power, it's always in complete harmony with His character. He isn't like one of the Greek gods, who could be moody or temperamental or decide to mess with our lives for fun. He is a God you can trust because He's "the same yesterday and today and forever" (Hebrews 13:8). So when troubles arise, you can rest in the knowledge that your trouble isn't outside of God's control, nor is it some sort of trick that He's playing on you to get His kicks.

Why God Permits Tribulation

You may be wondering, *If God is in control—if He really is sovereign—then why am I facing these problems? Why doesn't God just deliver me from my fears or cause the people in my life to change? Why does God let me suffer through these tribulations?*

You know, you might never know the exact answer to the question of *why* you're suffering. Yet here are some helpful thoughts to consider. One reason that suffering is part of this life is because God has a higher goal than just our temporal happiness or comfort. His goal is our eternal happiness and His glory. When God permits difficulties in our lives, it isn't because He hates us or is unable to stop bad things from happening. It's because He's interested in building our faith, changing our character, bringing us more joy, and freeing us from our fears. Could He free you from your fears? Yes. Will He free you? Yes, when it pleases Him to do so. In the meantime, He's using your fear to draw you to Himself and to change you. If you didn't struggle with these problems, you wouldn't see your need for Him. You see, God is interested in this change in you because He is going to be glorified because of it, and that's the goal of everything He does: His glory.

How We Can Grow Through Tribulation

The Bible speaks expansively about God's goals in our suffering:

- God permits troubles so that we'll experience His comfort and learn to comfort others and trust in Him and not ourselves (2 Corinthians 1:3-10).
- God permits tribulation so that we can grow in hope (Romans 5:3-5).
- God permits trials so that we will grow in holiness (Hebrews 12:10-11).
- Troubles are the seed-bed where faith grows (1 Peter 1:7).
- Experiencing God's help through our trials strengthens us (James 1:3-4).
- God wants our character to reflect Christ's (Romans 8:28-29).
- Troubles humble us and cause us to run to Jesus (1 Peter 5:5-7).

- Our suffering produces God-focused rejoicing (1 Peter 4:13).

Paul, who underwent extreme suffering for Christ during his whole life, wrote, "For momentary, light affliction is producing for us an eternal weight of glory far beyond all comparison" (2 Corinthians 4:17).

Look at the words that Paul uses to describe his suffering "momentary" and "light." And notice the words he uses to describe the benefits: "eternal weight of glory far beyond all comparison." "So the account stands in the view of Paul; and with this balance in favor of the eternal glory, he regarded afflictions as mere trifles, and made it the grand purpose of his life to gain the glory of the heavens. What wise man, looking at the account, would not do likewise?"[5]

Our suffering is producing something so incomparable that instead of fearing suffering, or fearing the suffering that our fear may bring us, the Bible tells us that we ought to rejoice in it! That's shocking, isn't it? But the truth is that we're being made fit for heaven. We're being prepared to experience the splendor, magnificence, honor, and happiness of the eternal world. Suffering does this for us, and learning to trust God in the storm is just what we need.

I'm not saying that you should purposely try to bring troubles upon yourself, or do whatever you can to keep your troubles coming. Rather, we need to realize that troubles are inevitable, and we shouldn't run or try to hide from them. We should face them in prayer and faith, believing that God will use them for our ultimate joy.

Examples of Growth Through Tribulation

The apostle Paul is not the only one who realized the benefit of troubles. Many other people through the ages have learned this as well. Madam Guyon, who was born in 1638 and persecuted for her faith, spent many years imprisoned in a dungeon lit only by a candle at mealtimes. She wrote this poem of her experience:

> A little bird I am,
> Shut from the fields of air;
> Yet in my cage I sit and sing
> To Him who placed me there;
> Well pleased a prisoner to be,
> *Because, my God, it pleases Thee*[6] (emphasis added).

After living through a childhood of hideous sexual and physical abuse in numerous foster care homes, Doris Van Stone, author of *No Place to Cry: The Hurt and Healing of Sexual Abuse*, wrote, "I can honestly say that there is nothing in my life I would change....I can say that I wouldn't change anything for this one reason: *God has been glorified through my suffering*"[7] (emphasis added).

I love the story of the founder of the Protestant Reformation, Martin Luther. In 1521 he was called before a tribunal and commanded to retract his writings. It certainly would have been understandable if Luther had done so, for the command had been issued by the emperor, and his disobedience would carry a death sentence. As Luther stood there, before church and government officials, he asked for a night to consider his answer. You can imagine the turmoil that raged in his heart during that dark night. Was it wrong to refuse to obey his emperor? Did God want him to die as a martyr? Were his beliefs really so different that he had to die for them? Why wasn't God protecting him? Why did he have to face this affliction? Can you imagine the confusion and fear that must have gripped his heart? After wrestling all night with his God, his fears, and his conscience, Luther met the next day with the commission. This is what he said:

> Unless you can prove from the Bible that I have made wrong statements, I cannot and I will not take back anything. My conscience is bound by the Word of God. Here I stand. I cannot do otherwise. God help me. Amen.

Luther's words have resounded down through the ages as millions of martyrs have stood before their persecutors and their fears. "Here I stand. I cannot do otherwise. God help me."

Luther was convinced that the sovereign God he served was able either to deliver him or give him the grace to face his own death. He knew that the only answer to his fear was faith in the God who ruled over all rulers, the God who had total control over his life.[8]

As you face your fears—fears of suffering, fears of failure, fears of trouble and tribulation—you can know for certain that the God who loved you enough to send His Son to die for you is still ruling all of the universe. If, in His loving plan, you have to bow before what appears to be a frowning providence, you can be sure that He's got your ultimate happiness at heart. He's working to free you from your worries—not by giving you freedom from trouble, but by arranging circumstances so that as you go through them you'll experience the truth that He is everything He says He is.

Confidence in God's Control

On the day before our daughter was born, my husband lost his job. I can remember the cold hand of fear that gripped my heart after he came home from work and shared the news. What were we going to do? How would we survive? What would happen to our little family? That night began a year-long lesson in trust. If you had asked me at the time if I knew what God was up to, I would have said, "No, and if you do, please tell me!" But now, in hindsight, I treasure that time as a very special lesson that came to me from the hand of my loving

Father. I had always been afraid that we "wouldn't make it financially." The fear that God wouldn't provide for us was something that I had always known but had never really dealt with. But when God, in His loving providence, arranged for my husband to lose his job, He made me stand face to face with the terror that I thought I could never face. I learned, during the difficult months that followed, how God could take care of us even if we didn't have all the money I thought we needed. Today I'm thankful for that lesson, for it serves as a constant and affirming reminder that God is reigning supreme over all and I can trust Him.

Is the truth of God's sovereignty just what Carol, Barbara, Dave, Nate, Jan, and you and I need? Of course it is. Carol needs to take comfort in knowing that God is in control of her church, and that He's protecting it and accomplishing His will there. Those who accuse and those who are accused are all in His grasp, and He won't allow the turmoil to continue one more moment than He pleases. Barbara needs to know that God is there, with her, in the midst of her tragedies and that He's going to use all her heartache for His glory and her good. She's already beginning to see that her life, as difficult as it has been, is a mighty tool in God's hands to bring others to His Son. Dave and Anne need to see that God is sovereign over life and death and that even though their hearts are being crushed, He has promised to be with them, both in life and in death. They can trust that God can heal her, if He chooses to do so. He may miraculously heal her in response to prayer or through her doctor's efforts. But, in the meantime, He's teaching them to trust and rely on Him in ways that they had never known.

Nate needs to realize that God brings calamity into our lives for our good, and the presence of calamity doesn't mean that we've somehow displeased God or missed His will. God delights in teaching us that we can make it, even in the worst-case scenarios. He's using this disaster to humble Nate's heart and redirect him. Jan is facing the consequences of her past life as she is afflicted with a virus that may ultimately overtake her. God is using her illness to free her from her fears and from the love of the world, and He's fitting her for heaven. He's teaching her that just as she has learned to trust Him for her salvation, she can trust Him day by day for her health and strength. With Him, she can face her greatest fear—death—with the knowledge that He will somehow be glorified through her life.

A Safe Harbor of Refuge

Do we need to embrace God's sovereignty as we face each of our fears? Yes, because it's only there that we'll find the peace that Jesus promised. Remember: In the world you'll have tribulation, but you can be of good cheer, the world isn't in control. "I have overcome the world" is Jesus' promise to you.

Remember too that God's sovereignty is a safe harbor in which we can take refuge. Consider Paul's words in the following Bible passage; ponder their import in your heart. This is the power of the sovereign King whom you serve:

> Who will separate us from the love of Christ? Will tribulation, or distress, or persecution, or famine, or nakedness, or peril, or sword? Just as it is written, "For Your sake we are being put to death all day long; we were considered as sheep to be slaughtered." But in all these things we overwhelmingly conquer through Him who loved us. For I am convinced that neither death, nor life, nor angels, nor principalities, nor things present, nor things to come, nor powers, nor height, nor depth, nor any other created thing, will be able to separate us from the love of God, which is in Christ Jesus our Lord."
> —Romans 8:35-39

For Further Thought

1. Write out the definition of *sovereignty* as given on page 126. Is the thought of God's sovereign rule something new to you? Do you find it comforting or troubling? Why?

2. After reviewing what God says about His sovereign rule on pages 127-128, choose the one fact that seems most difficult to believe and look up each of the references.

3. What does "man proposes but God disposes" mean to you? What does it mean in your particular circumstance?

4. In the table on page 140, list your four most common fears. On the other side of the table, write out how God's sovereignty might comfort you in light of your concerns.

Your Fears	Your Comfort in God
1.	1.
2.	2.
3.	3.
4.	4.

5. Jeremiah 10:23 says, "I know, O Lord, that a man's way is not in himself, nor is it in a man who walks to direct his steps." Charles Spurgeon called this "An Instructive Truth" and preached a sermon on it, part of which is quoted below. Allow God to comfort and encourage your heart through these words:

Child of God, will you, for a moment, reflect upon the overruling power of God even in the case of the most mighty and wicked of men? They sin grossly, and what they do is done of their own free will, and the responsibility for it lies at their own door. That we never can forget, for the free agency of man is a self-evident truth; but, at the same time, God is omnipotent, and He is still working out His wise designs, as He did of old, in the whirlwind of human wrath, in the tempest of human sin, and even in the dark mines of human ambition and tyranny, all the while displaying His sovereign will among men even as the potter forms the vessels on the wheel according to His own will.

This truth ought to be remembered by us, because it tends to take from us all fear of man. Why shouldst thou, O believer, be afraid of a man that shall die, or the son of man, who is but a worm? Thou art, as a child of God, under divine protection; so, who is he that shall harm thee while thou art a follower of that which is good? Remember that ancient promise, "No weapon that is formed against thee shall prosper; and every tongue that shall rise against thee in judgment thou shalt condemn. This is the heritage of the servants of the Lord" (Isaiah 54:17). The most powerful enemy of the Church can do nothing without God's permission. He can put a bit into the mouth of leviathan, and do with him as He pleaseth. The almighty God is Master and Lord even over the men who imagine that all power is in their hands.

And while this truth should banish our fear of man, it should also ensure our submission to the will of God. Suppose that the Lord allows Nebuchadnezzar to devastate the land that He gave to His people by covenant; it is God who permits it, therefore think not thou so much of the instrument employed by Him as of the hand in which that instrument is held. Art thou afflicted, poor soul, by some hard unkind spirit? Remember that God permits thee to be so tried, and be not angry with that which is only the second cause of thy trouble, but believe that the Lord permits this to happen to thee for thy good, and therefore submit thyself to Him.

This truth ought also to strengthen our faith. When fear goes, faith comes in. It is an easy matter to trust God when everything goes smoothly; but genuine faith trusts God in a storm.[9]

The Fear That Results in Blessings

"Fear of God is the one fear that dispels all others."
—JAY E. ADAMS[1]
Leader of the biblical counseling movement,
author, and pastor

*T*he music of the pipes and cymbals filled the air once again. Leaders had been called from every province to worship the golden statue that King Nebuchadnezzar had erected. As a sign of their allegiance to the king who ruled as a god, they bowed low before his statue. King Nebuchadnezzar looked with pride upon the men who had to bow at his word. As he did so, his advisers came to him with startling news. "Good king," they said, "there are three Jews that you have set up as administrators over the province of Babylon who refuse to bow before your statue!" The king was filled with rage. "Bring them to me!" he shouted.

The three young Hebrew men were brought before the king. He asked them, "Is this true? Do you dare to refuse my command? I'll give you another chance, but if you disobey, I will throw the three of you into the fiery furnace, and no one can save you then—not even your God!"

The young men, Shadrach, Meshach, and Abednego, had an astonishing answer for the king. They said,

> O Nebuchadnezzar, we do not need to give you an
> answer concerning this matter. If it be so, our God
> whom we serve is able to deliver us from the furnace
> of blazing fire; and He will deliver us out of your hand,
> O king. But even if He does not, let it be known to
> you, O king, that we are not going to serve your gods
> or worship the golden image that you have set up.
> —Daniel 3:16-18

Can you imagine the fear that must have filled the hearts of these three men as the king raged against them? "Make the fire even hotter!" he shouted. Were these men so courageous that the thought of being burned alive didn't alarm them? I doubt it, don't you? I can imagine that they had already decided that their death was a probable outcome of the king's order. They had probably talked and prayed together that God would help them to stand against the king and face their imminent deaths. Why were they willing to do this? Because they knew they were to fear God more than anything else in the world, even if that meant they had to disobey the king. This was a lesson that they had learned as they were exiled from their home in Judah for idolatry. The exile had taught them to fear and worship God alone. And so, even though their refusal to bow meant their probable execution, they weren't going to give in to the wicked king's demands.

As we read this story thousands of years later, it might not seem like they had that hard of a choice. After all, God did deliver them. But let's remember that they didn't have any assurance of what God was going to do. They didn't know whether He would deliver them or not. All they knew was that they had to fear Him more than they feared the king. Jesus echoed this same thought when He said, "I say to you, My friends, do not be afraid of those who kill the body and after that have no more that they can do. But I will warn you whom to fear: fear the One who, after He has killed, has authority to cast into hell; yes, I tell you, fear Him!" (Luke 12:4-5).

In your struggle to overcome your fears, the one factor that will most enable you to grow will be *the fear of God*. Let's take a few moments now to understand this different kind of fear, and then we'll see how it can be cultivated in our lives.

What Is the Fear of God?

Dr. Jay Adams defines the fear of God as "loving and respectful obedience toward Him."[2] Dr. Ed Welch, in his very helpful book, *When People Are Big and God Is Small*, writes,

> This fear of the Lord means *reverent submission that leads to obedience,* and it is interchangeable with "worship," "rely on," "trust," and "hope in." Like terror, it includes a clear-eyed knowledge of God's justice and His anger against sin. But this worship-fear also knows God's great forgiveness, mercy, and love....It causes us to submit gladly to His Lordship and delight in obedience. This kind of robust fear is the pinnacle of our response to God."[3]

The fear of the Lord is not the cringing terror of a slave who has displeased a demanding taskmaster. It doesn't drive us *away* from God; but rather *toward* Him, in humble obedience and worship. The Bible says that the devils have that cringing fear of God; they "shudder" before Him (James 2:19). But this isn't the fear that God wants His children to have. He does want you to know that He is holy, He is different, and that you can't fool Him. But He doesn't want that knowledge to drive you away from Him. He wants that knowledge to drive you toward Him— to cause you to flee to Him for mercy and grace. Spurgeon wrote,

> Between the fear of a slave and the fear of a child, we can all perceive a great distinction. Between the fear

of God's great power and justice which the devils
have, and that fear which a child of God has when he
walks in the light with his God, there is as much difference, surely, as between hell and heaven.[4]

Many people who struggle with fears and anxieties have a
distorted view of the Lord. This view causes them to focus more
on His wrath, His demands, His immensity, and His "uncontrollable Godness" at the exclusion of His other characteristics.
Whether they do so because they lived through a difficult childhood, had an abusive parent or spouse, or just because they
have a more timorous nature, the reality is that their terror is
more of a factor in their relationship with Him than delightful
awe. The balance that God wants us to embrace is one that
holds on to *all* of His qualities, not just some of them.

The terror of the Lord is an emotion that Satan will use to
keep you from your only source of help. He will continue to
point out your faults: how you've fallen short, how you're different from others, how God couldn't possibly love you. In the
Bible, Satan is called the "accuser of our brethren" (Revelation
12:10), and that's exactly what he is. He will tell you that you're
weaker than other Christians, you didn't have the right
upbringing, you don't have the right skills or temperament or
experience to be a strong believer. He will point out all the
possibilities for failure and tell you that the only smart move
for you is to give up.

In John Bunyan's timeless book *The Pilgrim's Progress* we see
an insightful illustration of this kind of fear. During a difficult
part of Pilgrim's journey towards the Celestial City, he meets
with a pair of men running towards him. Their names are Timorous and Mistrust. Christian asks them why they were running away. Timorous answers,

...that they were going to the City of Zion, and had got
up that difficult place; but, said he, "The further we go,

the more danger we meet with; wherefore we turned, and are going back again." "Yes," said Mistrust, "for just before us lie a couple of lions in the way, whether sleeping or waking we know not, and we could not think, if we came within reach, but they would presently pull us in pieces." Then said Christian, "You make me afraid, but whither shall I fly to be safe? If I go back to mine own country, that is prepared for fire and brimstone, and I shall certainly perish there. If I can get to the Celestial City, I am sure to be in safety there. I must venture. To go back is nothing but death; *to go forward is fear of death, and life everlasting beyond it. I will yet go forward*" (emphasis added).[5]

Isn't Bunyan's little illustration profound? The only way to overcome fear is to move toward God, toward everlasting life, toward the Celestial City. The only way for you and me to overcome the fears that haunt us and drive us to despair is to run, with all our might, towards the God who calls us. Perhaps, as you look at your circumstance, it seems as though there are lions waiting to devour you. Perhaps even your fear itself is threatening to swallow you up. The way to break free of your fear is not to run from it, but rather to press on in joyful obedience and faith in the face of it.

If my life wasn't so tumultuous, you might think, *I would be able to serve God. When things calm down, I'll obey Him.* Do you see the folly of hiding away from Him instead of finding Him as your Hiding Place? Our lives will always be beset on every side with terrors, difficulties, uncertainties, and grim prospects. We cannot shrink back from our duty to God because it is that duty, that awe-filled obedience, that will burst the chains of fear from our hearts and flood our souls with light.

The Benefits of Fearing God

The kind of fear that I'm talking about—the kind that the Scriptures command—is the fear that draws you toward Him, that causes you to fall down before Him in joyous worship, that keeps your heart continually focused on His will, come what may. The Bible says much about the benefits found in this kind of fear. Here are some verses for your consideration:

- "The fear of the Lord is the beginning *of wisdom*" (Psalm 111:10).
- "*How blessed* is the man who fears the Lord" (Psalm 112:1).
- "The fear of the Lord is the beginning *of knowledge* " (Proverbs 1:7).
- "In the fear of the Lord there is *strong confidence*" (Proverbs 14:26).
- "The fear of the Lord is *a fountain of life*" (Proverbs 14:27).
- "The fear of the Lord *leads to life*, so that one may *sleep satisfied, untouched by evil*" (Proverbs 19:23).
- "He will be the *stability of your times*, a *wealth of salvation, wisdom and knowledge*; the fear of the Lord *is his treasure*" (Isaiah 33:6).
- "I will put the fear of Me in their hearts so that *they will not turn away from Me*" (Jeremiah 32:40).

The advantages of developing this kind of fear are obvious. The fear of the Lord will provide the strength that you need to face and overcome your deepest fears. That's because God blesses this kind of fear. Through it He will empower you to become the kind of believer that you've always wanted to be.

The apostle Peter, who isn't generally thought of as a bastion of fearlessness, wrote the following to wives who were facing discord and persecution in their homes: "Do what is right," he said, "without being frightened by any fear" (1 Peter 3:6). Later in the same passage he also wrote, "Do not fear their intimidation, and do not be troubled, but sanctify Christ as Lord in your hearts" (verses 14-15). What is Peter saying to us? He's saying that we need to fear God more than we fear anything or anyone else. He's saying that even in the face of our gravest fears, we must fear God more and move ahead in faithful obedience.

We can't stop our hearts from pounding or our stomach from being tied up in knots. We can't control our physical symptoms. But we can, by God's power and grace, offer our joyful obedience to Him—and trust that He will give us confidence and calm in the midst of the storm.

Learning to Fear God

I hope that I've whetted your appetite for cultivating the fear of the Lord, and now I want to offer some practical steps that will help you get started today. In order to help you remember the steps for developing godly fear, I've developed an acrostic: FEAR GOD. Don't look at these steps as being in order of importance; I'm simply giving you a handy way of remembering them. In fact, you'll need to practice them simultaneously, rather than consecutively.

• **F**eed on His promises.

Etch them on your heart.

Adhere to His commands.

Rest and **R**ejoice in His love.

Go to Him in prayer.

Order your day for Him.

Depend on His strength.

Let's go letter by letter through the steps so that you can begin right now to strengthen your walk with Him.

Feed on His Promises

Many Christians who struggle with the wrong kind of fear usually focus on Bible verses about God's anger, wrath, and judgment. These aspects of God are in Scripture, but to have a correct and balanced perspective we should also spend time looking at the many wonderful promises of blessing from God. I've listed some below for you:

- He's promised to love you forever (Jeremiah 31:3).

- He's promised that He would never leave you (Hebrews 13:5).

- He's promised never to put you in a situation that's more than you can bear (1 Corinthians 10:13).

- He's promised to fill your heart with peace and joy (John 15:11; 16:24,33).

- He's promised to welcome all who come to Him (John 6:37).

- He's promised to hear all your prayers (Luke 11:9-10).

- He's promised to give you the strength you need for every situation (Philippians 4:13).

- He's promised to be a father to you by providing for you and protecting you (Genesis 22:14; Isaiah 64:8).

- He's promised to forgive all your sins (1 John 1:9).

- He's promised to keep you from all harm (Psalm 121:7; John 10:28).

- He's promised that you'll join Him in heaven (John 6:40; 14:3).

Etch Them on Your Heart

The only way that you'll be able to fight the attacks of fear or panic is with the help of God's Word. The Bible is called the "sword of the Spirit" (Ephesians 6:17), and with it the Holy Spirit can help us to slay the dragons of unbelief, doubt, and fear.

If you're like many people, memorizing Scripture can seem very difficult. Let me encourage you to choose one verse a week from the lists in this chapter and seek to memorize it. If you're a visual learner, rather than say the verse out loud over and over, why not write it down a number of times? You can also carry an index card with the verse on it and, whenever you have a free moment, read the verse or write it out again.

Adhere to His Commands

Adhering to the commands of God's Word will be of great benefit to you in overcoming your sinful fears. When you're tempted to flee from a difficult obedience, such as talking to an acquaintance about the Lord or helping someone who is in need, remember that the only power in heaven and earth that is strong enough to help you is God's. He's right there to help you obey Him, and the more that you practice each difficult obedience, the stronger you'll become. Remember that growing in holiness is just that—growing. Author David Powlison says that our spiritual growth is much like a yo-yo that's being used by a man walking up a flight of stairs. Our growth has ups and downs just like the yo-yo, but our general momentum is always upward, like the man going up the stairs.

Rest and Rejoice in His Love

For people who have overly sensitive consciences or who are filled with dread of God, resting and rejoicing seem almost impossible. *If I let down my guard, if I really think about rejoicing in Him, I'm afraid of what might happen. Maybe He will think that I'm not respecting Him. Maybe He will become angry.* The truth is that we're commanded to rest in His righteousness and love and to rejoice with happiness before Him. For instance, Psalm 37:7 says that we should "rest in the Lord and wait patiently for Him." And Paul told the Philippians to "rejoice in the Lord always" —not just once, but twice! (Philippians 4:4).

Go to Him in Prayer

As we saw in chapter 7, thankful prayer is one of the main keys to freeing your heart from worry. It's also the way that you'll be freed from the wrong kind of fear. Ask God to free you from your fears; tell Him what your concerns are, and remember to thank Him.

Order Your Day for Him

One problem with worry is that it stops us from doing the things we need to do. For instance, in the course of writing this book, I have sometimes felt overwhelmed and fearful. I've been afraid that I won't know how to say what needs to be said. I've been afraid that I won't be able to meet my deadlines. I've been afraid that my publisher won't like what I've written or that I'll be misunderstood. Then there's always the fear of the critics! But the more I think about my fears, the more time I waste, and in doing so, the more I fall behind.

Instead of letting fear and worry monopolize the limited time I have on my hands, I need to work...and leave the outcome in God's hands. The more fearful that you are about something that will happen in your day, the more necessary it is for you to order your day and complete what God has placed before you. If you're fearful of going to the grocery store, then go there first and get your fear out of the way. Schedule your time to show your desire to please God, and don't allow yourself time to worry or fret about what might happen if....

On page 153 is a schedule you can use. Look at the table on page 118 (in chapter 7). On that table you've prioritized your concerns—the tasks that you tend to worry about. Using the schedule on page 153, figure out the tasks you need to

Day	Task (DV)	Time Needed	Benefit
Monday			
Tuesday			
Wednesday			
Thursday			
Friday			
Saturday			
Sunday			

complete, how much time each task should take, and the benefits of completing that task.

Then offer the entire schedule to the Lord, acknowledging to Him that He is Lord over all schedules, and that this is what you want to accomplish—*unless He has other plans*. I've put the letters DV on the schedule, which stand for *Deo Volente*, which is Latin for "God willing." Remember that God will give you the strength to do whatever He has commanded you to do.

You'll see that I've completed a sample schedule for you so that you can get an idea of how to use it. I've also included a schedule in Appendix C on page 219 so you can copy it for personal use.

Day	Task (DV)	Time Needed	Benefit
Monday	Plan the meals for the week. Make a grocery list.	One hour	Better meals for the family.
	Pray for strength to go to the store.	Fifteen minutes	I'll remember that God promised to help me.
	Memorize one verse.		
Tuesday	Drive to the store. Remember to pray for strength and to thank Him.	Two hours	God will be pleased with my efforts at obedience. My family will be happy to have food to eat at home.
Wednesday	Write a letter to a friend, telling her what God is doing in my life.	One hour	My friend will be encouraged and God will get glory from my life.
Thursday	Clean the closets and start the laundry. Remember prayer!	Four hours	We'll have clothes to wear and I won't worry about the messy closets anymore.
Friday	Go for a walk and talk with God as I go. Review memory verse.	Half hour	I'll feel better and I won't feel like I'm hiding out anymore.
Saturday	Make breakfast for the family and suggest some recreation we could all do.	One hour	Taking time to be with the family and showing that I care for them will encourage them and give me an opportunity to show them what God is doing in my life.
Sunday	Go to church. Spend the day in prayer, praise, fellowship, and Bible memorization.	All day	I'll have the opportunity to hear God's Word and to fellowship with other believers.

Remember, this schedule is just a tool for you to use as you learn to fear God in the right way. Don't look at it as set in stone or feel that you've utterly failed if you don't accomplish everything on it. On the other hand, ask God for the strength to accomplish the goals you've set and trust that He will enable you to do them.

Depend on His Strength

The truth about overcoming fear or any other problem is that we can't do it on our own. I could fill all the pages of this book with charts, graphs, and page after page of witticisms, but without God's help, you and I could never really change at the core of our being. Let's look at some Scriptures that talk about God sharing His strength with us, and then we'll see how we can develop a dependent heart. I know I've listed a lot of verses, but I've done that so that you can be encouraged by God's truth. These verses would be good ones to etch on your heart as you grow in strength. The italicized portions reflect emphasis that's been added.

- "O Lord GOD, You have begun to show Your servant Your greatness and Your strong hand; *for what god is there in heaven or on earth who can do such works and mighty acts as Yours?*" (Deuteronomy 3:24).

- "Be strong and courageous, do not be afraid or tremble at them, for the Lord your God is the one who goes with you. *He will not fail you or forsake you*" (Deuteronomy 31:6).

- "Have I not commanded you? Be strong and courageous! Do not tremble or be dismayed, for *the Lord your God is with you wherever you go*" (Joshua 1:9).

- "Who is the King of glory? The Lord strong and mighty, the Lord mighty in battle" (Psalm 24:8).

- "Wait for the Lord; *be strong and let your heart take courage*; yes, wait for the Lord" (Psalm 27:14).

- "The name of the Lord is *a strong tower; the righteous runs into it and is safe*" (Proverbs 18:10).

- "*He gives strength to the weary, and to him who lacks might He increases power.* Though youths grow weary and tired, and vigorous young men stumble badly, yet those who wait for the Lord will *gain new strength*; they will mount up with wings like eagles, they will run and not get tired, they will walk and not become weary" (Isaiah 40:29-31).

- "Do not fear, for I am with you; do not anxiously look about you, for I am your God. *I will strengthen you, surely I will help you, surely I will uphold you* with My righteous right hand" (Isaiah 41:10).

- " 'My grace is sufficient for you, for *power is perfected in weakness.*' Most gladly, therefore, I will rather boast about my weaknesses, so that the power of Christ may dwell in me. Therefore I am well content with weaknesses, with insults, with distresses, with persecutions, with difficulties, for Christ's sake; *for when I am weak, then I am strong*" (2 Corinthians 12:9-10).

- "Be *strong in the Lord and in the strength of His might*" (Ephesians 6:10).

His Strength or Yours?

I know that most Christians long to experience God's strength and live in total dependence upon Him. What's hard is trying to discern what dependent living actually looks like. Does it mean that I don't move my hand unless God moves it?

Does it mean that I have to wait for God to give me some kind of power transfusion before I can obey? No, the truth is that if you belong to Christ, you've already been given all the power that you need. The Holy Spirit who indwells all believers is daily empowering you to obey. Your part in depending upon God is to ask for His strength, obey in His might, praise Him when you're successful, and thank Him when you're not. In other words, depending on God's strength means living every step of the way with the awareness that you need His help. And, even if you fail to do so, God will redeem the experience and use it for your ultimate good.

The Promise of Blessings and Freedom

I know that I've given you a lot to think about in this chapter. I've tried to encourage you with the truth that the only way you can overcome your fears is to embrace the one fear that's stronger than any other: the fear of God. I hope that you'll take the time to memorize the FEAR GOD acrostic and that you'll begin to experience the freedom from fear that the fear of God will bring.

In closing, I'd like to share a short quote from Charles Spurgoon's sermon, "A Fear to Be Desired":

> When the heart is filled with the fear of God there is no room for other fears. The fear of God must reign supreme in the heart. When it does, it drives out all other fears that would enslave us….This fear leans toward the Lord. When thou really knowest God, thou shalt be thrice happy if thou dost run toward Him, falling down before Him, worshipping Him with bowed head yet glad heart, all the while fearing toward Him, and not away from Him. Blessed is the man whose heart is filled with that holy fear which inclines his steps in the way of God's commandments, inclines his heart to seek after God, and inclines his

whole soul to enter into fellowship with God, that he may be acquainted with Him, and be at peace.[6]

Wouldn't you like to experience the blessings of fearing God? Wouldn't you like to experience sweet fellowship with the one who loves you more than you could ever imagine? The blessings of fearing God aren't for someone else; if you are God's child, then the blessings are intended for you. Like Christian in *The Pilgrim's Progress,* you can decide to lean towards Him in spite of your difficult circumstances. You will find God ready to welcome you with open arms, waiting as a loving Father, ready to bring you closer to Him.

For Further Thought

1. Write out each principle of the F-E-A-R G-O-D acrostic below.

F

E

A

R

G

O

D

2. Take time to meditate on each of the principles above. What steps can you take in order to grow in the right kind of fear? Try to be as specific as you can, with practical ideas or plans.

3. Do you need to write out a schedule that will help you to accomplish the tasks that fill you with worry or fear? Copy the schedule on page 217 and begin to work on it today.

4. Try to explain the difference between the right and wrong kinds of fears.

The Opposite of Fear: Love

"The enemy of fear is love; the way to put off fear, then, is to put on love."[1]

—JAY E. ADAMS

$\mathcal{P}$am had walked with Christ for nearly 30 years, but because she found herself mired quite often in depressions, she had begun to wonder if she was really a believer. She had started to look at every little thing in her life and examine it for signs that she might not be a Christian. She also wanted to love God, but she found herself dreading Him. Every time she read a verse in Scripture that spoke of obedience, she somehow interpreted it to mean that she wasn't saved. Because of her doubts, she was consumed with thoughts about punishment and how she had let God down too many times to be forgiven again. This led to more and more severe depressions which, in turn, caused her to more seriously doubt her salvation. Even though Pam knew that Christ died for all her sins, she had trouble believing that His forgiveness would extend to her constant daily weaknesses.

Margot had been struggling with a particular fear for over a year. Over that period of time, she had become more and more afraid to drive on the freeway, which necessitated her driving on crowded side streets. This made her responsibilities as the mother of two daughters increasingly more difficult. She was having trouble getting the girls to their engagements. Her girls were consistently late to their team sports and club activities. Frequently they weren't allowed to participate because of tardiness. She had asked to be excused from her responsibilities at Sunday school because she couldn't arrive on time, creating an inconvenience for her co-teacher. As time went on, Margot's fears continued to close in on her, and her ability to function got more and more constrained.

A number of years ago my husband and I were invited to a relative's wedding. Since I hadn't seen this part of the family for a long time and I was concerned about how they would perceive me, I was filled with fear for days. What would I wear? What if I was overdressed? Underdressed? What if I didn't know what to say? I wanted to seem clever and intelligent. I wanted them to approve of me. As the day drew nearer, I became irritable and nervous. When the day finally arrived, I was filled with dread and insecurity. During the reception, as I was being introduced to friends of the family, I found I was so filled with fear that my mind was blank. I couldn't think of anything to say. When someone introduced a family friend, "This is so-and-so, he lives in Las Vegas," all I could think to respond was, "Las Vegas is hot." Needless to say, that was the end of my being introduced around. I went back to my corner table humiliated and mortified. Where could I run and hide from my imbecility? *"Las Vegas is hot?"* Why would I say something as inane as that? Why was I unable to carry on a decent conversation? What was the problem?

You can see that fear was a significant problem for Pam, Margot, and me. How does a person overcome the fears that restrict one's actions, that obstruct one's conversations and even relationships? In a previous chapter we looked at one facet of overcoming a specific fear, the fear of man. We learned that the only way to overcome the fear of man was to cultivate a fear of God. Now we'll focus on the weapon in God's mighty arsenal that helps us to eliminate fear: love.

All You Need Is Love

When you think about fear, you might suppose that the opposite of fear is confidence or peace. You might think that what Pam, Margot, and I needed was better self-esteem. But the Bible says something quite different—it teaches that what we need isn't more self-love, but rather more love for others. That's because the opposite of fear isn't confidence or peace; *the opposite of fear is love.* The only way for Margot or Pam or me to overcome our fears is to learn to love more than we fear. And that's because the only power strong enough to eliminate fear is love: love for God and others. That's what the apostle John taught us in 1 John 4:18: "There is no fear in love; but perfect love casts out fear, because fear involves punishment, and the one who fears is not perfected in love."

Let's look closely at John's advice about overcoming fear and try to see how it works to slay this mighty dragon.

The Source of Love

So that we can better understand what John says about fear and love, we need to look at the passage surrounding 1 John 4:18. In that portion of Scripture he is speaking primarily about our love for God and being free from the dread of Him. Let's consider the whole passage as paraphrased in The Living Bible:

> We know how much God loves us because we have felt his love and because we believe him when he tells us that he loves us dearly. God is love, and anyone who lives in love is living with God and God is living in him. And as we live with Christ, our love grows more perfect and complete; so we will not be ashamed and embarrassed at the day of judgment, but can face him with confidence and joy, because he loves us and we love him too. We need have no fear of someone who loves us perfectly; his perfect love for us eliminates all dread of what he might do to us. If we are afraid, it is

for fear of what he might do to us, and shows that we
are not fully convinced that he really loves us. So you
see, our love for him comes as a result of his loving us
first.

—1 John 4:16-19

The kind of love John refers to here isn't merely the love that's common to most people. This powerful love comes from only one source: God. Although all good gifts come from God by His common grace (including the love that unbelievers have for one another), the kind of love John is talking about here is a love that is experienced only in a personal relationship with God. It's as we're drawn to Him and we enter into fellowship with Him that we experience the powerful fear-defeating love that is His alone. We can see the differences between a relationship based on fear and one based on love by considering the difference between being judged by a stranger and judged by a father. In this way we'll be better able to understand how love can cast out fear.

God as a Judge

I can't imagine a prospect more frightening than standing before a judge who is a stranger to me. Knowing that my actions are about to be judged by another who is not related to me or who doesn't love me would be terrifying. I would not feel at all comfortable with the prospect of receiving a punishment or verdict from a person who may not really know or care about me. My life determined by someone else? Someone who probably doesn't love or know me?

Now, an earthly judge doesn't know a person's innermost thoughts or motives like God does. So, the thought of standing before the throne of the Great Judge of the whole earth, with only my feeble and tainted attempts at goodness to recommend me, is even more terrifying. There is absolutely nothing we can hide from God, and it's frightening to think what would happen if we were to get the punishment we really deserve—a punishment that, for Christians, has already been paid by Jesus' death on the cross.

God as My Father

Contrast the prospect of standing before a judge with that of standing before a holy Father with whom you have relationship. Although His holiness is perfect and completely different from yours, it's His holiness that guides His every thought and action toward you and causes Him to respond to you in mercy and compassion. Now, imagine if you will, that you have a perfect Elder Brother that has always pleased your Father. You know that He's never done anything that offended your Father and that His relationship with your Father has never been abated in any way. Your Elder Brother has also offered to take your place before your Father's gaze because He knows that He has pleased His Father in everything and He loves you perfectly, as well. You can hide behind Him and know that you're perfectly safe from any wrath or judgment.

There's quite a difference between the two scenarios, isn't there? What is the essence of that difference? Love and relationship. It's this kind of love, springing from the Father and the Son, into which all believers can hide themselves. It's a response to this kind of love that will vanquish all fear of being punished. He loves us dearly, and we can be confident and joyful of that at the day of judgment. When we've been convinced of His love we will no longer be filled with the "dread of what He might do to us" any more than we dread what He will do to His beloved Son. This love draws us towards Him and others. It overcomes the dread that would send us running from relationships in terror. God is not only the Judge of the whole earth; He is also your loving Father.

God Is the Author of This Love

The wonderful news is that this kind of love isn't something that we have to work up all on our own, but rather it is a "result of his loving us first" (1 John 4:19 TLB). This love comes to us because of God's choice to pour His love into our hearts, as Romans 5:5 says, "The love of God has been poured out within our hearts through the Holy Spirit who was given to us." So, in the context of 1 John 4, John's concern was that we shouldn't be in dread of God, but rather, in response to His love, love Him in return. It is this love, which flows from Him, that is the only love strong enough to eliminate the fear of punishment.

Changing from Fear to Love

Pam, whose depressions I mentioned at the beginning of this chapter, grew as she meditated daily upon God's love for her. She began to see that He loved her in the face of her sin. She saw that He was pleased with her because He was pleased with His Son and she had put her trust in Christ and His perfection. Whenever a troubling thought entered her mind, saying, "You aren't really saved. A person who is really saved doesn't sin like you do," she remembered what John wrote and said to herself, "I'm not relying on my own goodness. I'm relying on the love that God has for me. Because He says that He loves me, I can trust that He will bring me safely through this time of doubt." She began to judge her thoughts by all of Scripture, not just those verses that tormented her. She still struggled with sin, but she realized that she also had a Savior who had taken care of her sins.

Pam took significant steps forward when she saw that her preoccupation with her sins was preventing her from loving God because she was spending all her time in doubt-filled intro-spection when she could have been serving others out of love for God. When she found herself mired down in a slough of doubt, she would remind herself of God's love, trust that He would be faithful to His Word and love her to the end, and then she would look for opportunities to serve others. In this way she practiced the truth that God's love for her was the only power strong enough to overcome her fears and doubts.

Pam began to meditate on verses such as 1 John 4:18 and Romans 8:15: "You have not received a spirit of slavery leading to fear again, but you have received a spirit of adoption as sons by which we cry out, 'Abba! Father!'" She studied verses on the Fatherhood of God, dwelling on the truths they taught:

- Isaiah 9:6—The eternal Father humbled Himself and came to us as a child to bring us His power, peace, and counsel.

- Galatians 4:6-7—God has adopted us into His family so that we can call Him "Abba." *Abba* is a term of endearment that speaks of an intimate relationship between a child and father. In New Testament times slaves were not allowed to use this term to address the head of the house, but dear children were invited to.

- 1 John 3:1—It's because of the Father's great love that we're called the children of God—and that's exactly what we are. It's not because of our goodness, but His alone.

- Luke 15:18-24—In the story of the prodigal son, God demonstrated His love for erring children by welcoming to His home a child who had no right to it or claim on righteousness.

If you, like Pam, have struggled with the assurance of whether or not you're really God's child, then there are some steps you can take to overcome your struggles. Of course, the first step is discerning whether or not you really are a Christian. Have you believed that Jesus Christ is the Son of God and that He lived a perfect life and died for your sin? If you have believed this and trusted Him for salvation, asking Him to forgive your sins and to bring you into His family, then you are His. If you're unsure about this, then you'll want to see Appendix A at the back of this book.

If, however, you know that you have trusted Christ for your salvation but constantly find yourself struggling with doubt, let me encourage you to take the following steps:

- Pray that God will help you see how much He loves you. Don't expect Him to necessarily cause you to "feel" something special during this prayer time. I'm not saying that feeling or experiencing God's love is bad; it's just not something we're ever told to pray for. Rather, ask Him to open your eyes to His Word and the work that He's done in your life.

- Challenge your troubling thoughts with answers from God's Word. Think particularly about God's love as described in the chart here. (You can also ask yourself the questions found in Appendix B on page 217). Fill in the blanks at the bottom portion of the chart with your fearful thoughts, and then use a concordance or the verses in this book to help you remember God's love.

Fearful Thoughts	Faithful Thoughts About God's Love for Me
I'm not sure I'm saved.	God has invited me to trust Him and believe. Because He loves me, He has promised that if I come to Him, He will not cast me out (Matthew 11:28-30, John 6:37).
I still struggle with sin so much that I can't believe that I'm really saved (John 3:16).	All believers struggle with sin (1 John 1:8). God's love is strong enough to overcome my sin. Christ's love bore the punishment for all my sin and His perfect record is now mine (Romans 5:8-10,18-19).

I'm afraid to die.	Because of His great love, Jesus Christ has conquered death by suffering through it for my sake (Hebrews 2:14-15). He's gone before me and promised to guide me safely to Him (John 14:1-3). He has promised to give me eternal life (John 6:29,37-40).
I've failed Him too many times.	Although my heart may condemn me, God's love is stronger than my heart (John 10:29-30; 1 John 3:20). He's promised to forgive my sin when I ask (1 John 1:9), and I believe that He's too loving and incapable of lying to me (Numbers 23:19).
Other people don't struggle like I do.	God hasn't commanded me to compare my walk with others (2 Corinthians 10:12). It's because of His great love that I still face struggles and because of His great love that I'll ultimately succeed (Romans 8:28-29).

- Remember that God has promised to care for you, no matter how tempted or tried you are, and that His love is too strong to leave you alone (Psalm 23; 1 Corinthians 10:13; Hebrews 13:5).

- Experiencing doubts doesn't mean that you aren't a believer. All believers struggle with doubts, and God invites us to come to Him in spite of our doubts. Our faith is based on God's character and not our feelings about our faith. God alone can hold us during our times of doubt and He invites us to cast all our cares on Him.[2]

- Seek to rejoice and be thankful in every situation, especially the most difficult ones, knowing that God is at work in your life because of His great love (Romans 8:28-29; Ephesians 5:20; 1 Thessalonians 5:16,18).

- Confess your sins of fear, worry, and unbelief. Thank God for His promised forgiveness (1 John 1:9).

- Seek to be obedient out of joyful gratitude (Romans 12:6-21).

Using steps like these, Pam was able to grow in her trust and obedience as she meditated on and embraced God's amazing love for her. She learned to rejoice in the fact that God's love for her wasn't based on what she did, but rather on His holiness and sovereign choice. She learned that she could rest in His goodness, and so can you.

Overcoming Fear by Loving Others

Since our relationship to God influences all other relationships and is the most important relationship of all, it is proper to broaden the application of John's principle of love casting out fear to all other relationships as well.

Let's look again at John's words: "There is no fear in love; but perfect love casts out fear" (1 John 4:18). We've already seen how God's love for us can eliminate our dread of judgment and can cause love to spring up in our heart for Him. Love can also help us to overcome fear in our relationships with others. Let's consider how Margot's love for her children could overcome her fear of driving on the freeway.

Margot's fear began after an incident she had with a flat tire. She had been traveling at a high speed and her tire had blown out, causing her to lose control of the car for a few moments. Thankfully, she was able to slow down and pull over to the shoulder, but then she had to get out and attempt to change the tire. She was very concerned about her children, who were in the car, and about the danger that they were exposed to. Several large trucks drove by her at very close range as she worked on the tire, and she got back into the car and cried from fear. Finally a helpful young man stopped, fixed her tire, and she was on her way. But the terror that she felt continued on for hours. As the days went by, she became more and more afraid. She drove more slowly, which caused her to be harassed by drivers who wanted to travel the speed limit.

Eventually, Margot felt that driving on the freeway was just too terrifying. She figured out how to get to her destinations using side streets, and even that began to bother her. Because she drove slowly and the side streets required extra time, she was consistently late to all her appointments. This led her to excuse herself from more and more activities. Margot's children and her husband were distressed by this change in her, but nothing they said or did could help her to overcome her fears. What did she need to do?

Margot was surprised to learn that the way to overcome her fears was through love. She started by reading and meditating upon verses about serving others:

- "In everything, therefore, treat people the same way you want them to treat you" (Matthew 7:12). Margot wanted others to understand her problems and to help her. God's priority for her, however, was to understand her daughters' needs and to help them.

- "Greater love has no one than this, that one lay down his life for his friends" (John 15:13). Beginning to drive on the freeway again was a sacrifice for Margot. She had to face the reality that she might, in fact, have another flat tire or even end up in an accident. For her, laying down her life meant being willing to face these dangers for the sake of the family she loved.

- "Be devoted to one another in brotherly love...persevering in tribulation" (Romans 12:10,12). Part of Margot's being devoted to her family was that she had to persevere in the tribulation of traveling on the freeway. She realized that God could help her persevere, even when she felt afraid of driving, and that He had given her the love that she needed to serve her family.

- "Owe nothing to anyone except to love one another....Love does no wrong to a neighbor; therefore love is the fulfillment of the law" (Romans 13:8,10). Margot's decision to stop driving caused problems for her daughters. They were unable to attend their clubs or participate in sports. Her fears were causing her to do wrong to her neighbor (in this case, her daughters), and the way to overcome her fear was to replace it with love for her daughters.

Putting God's Truth into Practice

The Change in Margot's Life

How could Margot triumph over the fear that was controlling her? How could she break free of the chains that bound her to her home? Romans 12:21 teaches, "Do not be overcome by evil, but overcome evil with good." She could overcome the evil (the sinful fear that kept her fettered to her home) by doing good. The good that she needed to do was to believe, in faith, that God would protect and help her. She couldn't overcome her fears by simply thinking about them or by wishing that she were free. In fact, when she thought about her fears, they simply became worse. She had to decide to do what was right, *no matter how she felt.*[3] She had to take action. She had to overcome evil by doing the good that presented itself to her: in this case, fulfilling her responsibilities as a wife and mother.

Margot also needed to learn that her life was in God's control. She had to realize that if something did go wrong, she could trust God to use the situation for good in her life. God hasn't promised to keep us from trials; rather, He has promised to use our trials for our good and His glory.

Margot spent time in prayer, rehearsing God's promises about how we can benefit from trials. She then starting driving short distances on the freeway. Each time she went out, she increased the distance. As she did so, she kept her thoughts focused on God's goodness by listening to praise tapes in her car. She also asked her husband if he would purchase a cell phone for her to use in case of an emergency, which he gladly did. Ultimately, Margot resolved that she would drive more and more on the freeway, regardless of her feelings, and that she would trust God to give her the strength she needed along the way. In time, she found herself back in the driver's seat again. She still felt fearful from time to time, but she kept in mind that her love for God and her family was more important that her fear of an accident. In this way, she learned in very practical daily experience to overcome evil with good.

Can you see how the love of Christ can control us? (2 Corinthians 5:14). Margot learned that because Christ was willing to die for her and to face the greatest fear of all—death and separation from God—that she should "no longer live for [herself], but for Him who died and rose again on [her] behalf" (verse 15). She also taught her children that they could serve God in spite of their fears.

The Change in My Life

Recently I had another opportunity to visit with a formerly estranged segment of my family. Before the visit I started to worry about all the usual concerns: What would I wear? What would I say? But this time, instead of fearing the people and their opinions of me, I asked God to help me love them more than I feared them. I wanted to minister to them, understand them, and let them know that I was a believer; so I prayed that God would help me to love them. Because love is stronger than fear, it overshadowed my heart and enabled me to be genuinely interested in their lives. I didn't worry about what I said or didn't say; I didn't care whether they approved of me or not. That's because I had become more concerned about loving them than I was worried about them loving me. As a result, I was able to be friendly and kind, and I found that I really did care for them.

God Makes It All Possible

The only way that we can cultivate the kind of love we need for God and others is by experiencing God's love. We know He loves us because He has chosen us; we've been made His sons and daughters through the sacrifice of Jesus Christ (Galatians 3:26). Because we have peace and acceptance from Him, we are free to love Him and others the way that He calls us to.

Also, as we go through life, we will experience different challenges that may open the door to fears. In fact, God will sometimes place us right in the middle of a circumstance that is tailor-made to confront our fears. He does this because He loves us and wants to bring light and life to every part of our heart, especially those places that we've kept hidden for so many years.

How can we love the way that God wants us to? It's possible because God first loved us. We can love because He first loved us; and as we spend time in prayer, meditation, and fellowship at the spring of love that flows unceasingly from His throne, we are cleansed, strengthened, and emboldened to throw ourselves unreservedly on His mercy. A sip of His pure love enables us to love others with a sacrificial love—a love that says, *I might suffer harm; I might have to face fearful circumstances; but I can love and serve you because of God's great love for me.*

Although the first step down the path of freedom from fear towards loving service might seem intimidating, you can be emboldened to take it as you remember God's great love for you. He'll be there with you all the way, enfusing you with His strong and liberating love, and teaching you that love is, after all, stronger than fear.

For Further Thought

1. Read Matthew 10:26-31. What is the relationship between the fear of man, the fear of God, and trust in His providential care? How does knowing that God cares even for the birds encourage you to love Him?

2. What is the difference between a holy fear of God and dread of Him?

3. Spurgeon said, "Dear heart, God is your best Friend, your choicest love."[4] Do you think of God in that way? What stops you?

4. If some sin has stopped you from thinking of God as "your best Friend," you can confess that sin and be made clean before Him. If you are stopped by your doubts, speak with Him about them (He knows them already anyway) and ask Him to show you the truth. If you are afraid that He will allow you to experience trials, recognize that He will allow only that which will change you for your own good, freedom, and joy, as well as for His own glory. Write a few words below about the good that has come out of past difficult circumstances, and thank God for what He has done.

5. What responsibilities are you neglecting because of fear? How would love overcome those fears? What steps do you need to take to overcome evil with good? Be specific here about the tasks you need to do. (For instance, Margot needed to start driving on the freeway again.) God will encourage and free you as you seek to faithfully obey Him out of love, no matter how you feel. Your feelings of fear may or may not diminish after a short time, but that's not the point. The point is to obey God out of love and to love others the way that He's loved you. In that you'll find great peace and freedom, no matter what your emotions do.

CHAPTER

I I

Growing Strong
in Grace

"Contrary to a common misconception,
we do not earn or forfeit God's blessings
in our daily lives based on our performance."[1]

—JERRY BRIDGES
Author and leader in The Navigators

*I*n the part of Southern California where I live, we have a ground fog from time to time. This fog develops during the night and on some mornings it's so thick that the tree in my front yard has disappeared. On other mornings, I can see the close-by range of foothills blanketed with silver and lavender hues, with the purplish summits seeming to gradually vanish in the misty distance. The fog softens harsh lines, subdues brilliant colors, and seems to quiet the din of our fast-paced existence. It's as though a child's blanket has been wrapped around our harried lives. On some days, I enjoy the fog.

The fog is beautiful at times, but at other times it can be treacherous, closing down the airports and creating traffic snarls. It can be perilous for those on our local freeways, because as you go uphill or downhill, what appears to be a clear roadway can suddenly become obscured in fog, causing all other traffic before and behind them to disappear. On the mornings when I have to go out and I need to see beyond my windshield, I find myself wishing that the fog would vanish.

A Clear View of God

Our understanding of God is, in some ways, like the view from my front window on a foggy morning. For most of us, our understanding of God's nature is shrouded in a misty haze of misconceptions, misunderstandings, unfamiliarity, and unbelief. For me, there have been times that it seemed that the fog had lifted, and just when I was getting used to the view, it settled back down again and I was unsure of what I saw. At other times, I have gotten an unclouded glimpse of God, and in those moments, I realize that my previous assumptions about who He is need to be amended.

Don't get me wrong. I'm not saying that God hides behind clouds or plays games with us. Like the tree in my yard or the foothills close by, the problem isn't that the reality or truth isn't there for me to see; the problem lies in my inability to see because of the fog. Likewise, my ability to comprehend God is frustrated by frailty, faulty preconceptions, misunderstandings, and the unbelief resident in my heart. It's as though there is a constant fog on my glasses. Yes, my understanding of God's character is clouded at best. As the apostle Paul says, in this present age, "we see in a mirror dimly...[we] know in part" (1 Corinthians 13:12).

How different do you think life would be if you and I had a clear and accurate view of God? That would be better than wandering in the fog of any incorrect perceptions we might have of God, wouldn't it? How would knowing Him *as He is* rather than *how we suppose Him to be* impact our struggles with fear, anxiety, and worry? Knowing God *as He is* is a mighty weapon in our ability to overcome fear.

We've already looked at the character of God in several places in this book. We've talked about His holiness, His compassion, His sovereignty, and His Fatherly disposition toward us. I've purposely spent time focusing our attention on Him because, in some measure, fear invariably flows out of a blurred image of who God is and what He's like. And, in my experience, one of the most elusive facets of God's nature is His *grace.*

So, in this chapter, we're going to look at His grace and see if we can lift the fog a little, or at least offer a paper towel to wipe off those lenses. Although we'll never be able to perfectly comprehend Him *as He is* (because He is so "other"), we can at least grow in our comprehension as much as is possible through the enlightenment of the Holy Spirit and the Scriptures.

Understanding God's Grace

Let's think for a moment about the definition of the word *grace.* I'm sure you've heard it defined as "God's unmerited favor." Yes, grace is God's unmerited favor, but that definition leaves out an important fact: It's His unmerited favor *to those who deserve only His wrath.* Grace is God's kindness and blessing on those who by their nature and their action deserve anything but.

Ephesians chapter 2 tells us, "By grace you have been saved through faith; and that not of yourselves, it is the gift of God; not as a result of works, so that no one may boast" (Ephesians 2:8-9).

It's because of God's kindness and goodness alone that you and I are saved from our sins. It is not by any works that we can do or even good works that we can add to His; it is God's work alone that saves. I'm thankful for that truth, and I'm sure you are, too.

Since all Christians believe in God's grace, why is it important for me to talk about it here? It seems as though it's just a given: Yes, we're saved by grace. The reason we need to revisit this is because of our narrow understanding of it. We tend to see grace solely as it pertains to our salvation and are inclined to miss it when it comes to our life after salvation. In other words, we believe that God saves us by *grace,* but our growth and perseverance after salvation is by our *works.* However, as Jerry Bridges writes, "We are not only saved by grace, but we also live by grace every day. This grace comes through Christ, 'through whom we have gained access by faith into this grace in which we now *stand.*'"[2]

Let's take the definition of grace that's written above and enlarge it for illustration's sake: Grace is God's unmerited favor to those who have been saved *and still, in their own strength, deserve only His wrath* but have His favor instead. That changes things a bit, doesn't it? We know that before we're saved we deserve judgment. But what about after we're saved? Do we still need His grace to stand before Him? Please pause and think with me. I'm not denigrating the truth that we're now in Christ, and because of that, God is now perfectly pleased with us. The Bible clearly teaches that because we're in Christ, we won't ever suffer God's wrath. It's settled. Yet you and I need God's grace *just as much* now as we did before we became saved. We must never rely on our performance, whether we think it's good or bad, because our performance is always stained by sin.

Resting in God's grace will help you to get rid of any fears you might have about how God perceives your performance. Gloria, a young college student, thought that if she failed to spend at least 15 minutes in prayer every morning before leaving her home, an accident would befall her. She thought that God's blessing or grace in her life rested on the weight of her prayers. She thought that God couldn't or wouldn't protect her unless she first spent time in prayer. As a result, she missed the joy and blessing of prayer and saw it as a kind of payoff for God's protection. In a very real sense, she felt that she had to earn God's Fatherly care and thus she missed the joy of grace.

Louise believed that if she spoke in a negative way, such as saying that she felt like she might be getting sick, God wouldn't be able to protect her from illness. She believed that her words were more powerful than God's desire to bless her, more powerful than His grace. She missed the joy of grace and her days were spent in self-focused fear and introspection: Had she said or thought anything that might bring an affliction upon her? Like Gloria, she believed that although her salvation was by grace, her walk with God was now based on her own performance.

Andrea would awaken every morning under a canopy of guilt. She would lay in bed and think about the previous day's actions until she remembered some way that she had failed the Lord. Although she would do the right thing by confessing these sins, she would spend the rest of the day trying to feel good about herself and her efforts to please God. She longed for a day when she could be confident that God approved of her performance. Although all Christians should long for holiness, she longed for something else: the ability to stand before God and know that she was guiltless *on her own merit*. She wrongly perceived that God sat in heaven with a score card in hand, marking pluses and minuses on it at the end of each day. She dreaded the thought that someday all the minuses would outweigh the pluses and God's judgment would come crashing down. The joy of relishing God's grace was missing from her life, and she found her faith filled with fear, labor, and self-disgust.

Andrea needed to see that God's grace rested on her not because of her own performance or her ability to do right, but because she was in His Son. The truth is that no matter how many pluses she piled up on her record in heaven, there never would be enough to outweigh even one sin. Aside from that, she had missed the truth that the biggest plus ever written was hers in the cross of Christ. It was this plus that had already offset all her sin.

When We Forget God's Grace

Can you see how a misunderstanding of God's grace brought fear to Gloria, Louise, and Andrea? These women had failed to see the truth that God has already determined His disposition toward His children, and it is a disposition filled with grace. That doesn't mean, of course, that God doesn't discipline Christians, a truth that we'll look at later in this chapter. In fact, discipline itself is a sign of God's loving care (Hebrews 12:5-11). Living in His grace also doesn't mean that we don't suffer the effects of life in a sin-cursed world. We sin, others sin against us, and our physical bodies eventually wear out and die. But as far as God's favor resting on our lives, that decision has already been made: God is going to bless us. That means whenever difficulties or trials come, we can sing, "...Christ hath regarded my helpless estate and has shed His own blood for my soul."[3]

Each of these three women knew they were saved by God's grace, but they mistakenly thought that God's grace was something that had to be earned on an ongoing basis. There were two key truths they had overlooked: First, they failed to realize that even on their good days they still weren't perfect enough to earn God's favor. And second, they missed the truth that on their bad days God's disposition toward them hadn't changed one whit. God's grace is a constant facet of His character: It never changes. Once He determines to love you, He will always love you, no matter what (see Psalm 102:27-28; Malachi 3:6; Hebrews 13:8; James 1:17).

If you think that God's love for you depends on your actions, if you think that He's sitting in heaven waiting for you to make a mistake so He can pull the rug out from under you, if you believe that He needs something from you in order to bless you, then your heart will be filled with fear. Contrast these befogged views of God's grace with these words from Psalms:

> As far as the east is from the west, so far has He
> removed our transgressions from us. Just as a father
> has compassion on his children, so the Lord has com-
> passion on those who fear Him. For He Himself
> knows our frame; He is mindful that we are but dust.
> —Psalm 103:12-14

What do these verses tell you about God's attitude towards you? He has removed all your sin, even those sins that you have committed today. He has compassion on you just like a father has compassion on his child. What else do these verses tell us? That He knows our frame or our nature; He knows that we are weak and frail.

Recently I was rocking my little grandson, Wesley. We were singing "Jesus Loves Me This I Know," and when we got to the part that says, "We are weak, but He is strong," I rephrased the line and said, "Wesley is weak, but Jesus is strong." As I looked at little Wesley and thought about those words, it was easy for me to see how he was weak and needed Christ's strength. Then I realized that I was weak as well. Even though I felt strong, sit-ting there holding this little child, I knew that my strength was like a vapor compared to the strength that I needed. Only God's grace is strong enough to enable me to stand against all the temptations and trials of this world and my weak nature. His grace infuses me with power—not a power that I could ever earn, but one that's mine because of His love.

The Greatness of God's Grace

Can you see how wrong beliefs about God's grace can create fear? The fear that "something bad is going to happen" flows out of a flawed perspective of God's love. The fear that a trial is about to overwhelm you has its genesis in a small view of God's grace. Here are some truths and verses for you to etch on your heart about the unchangeable character of God's gracious love (remember our FEAR GOD acronym in chapter 9, in which the letter *E* stands for Etch Them on Your Heart):

- God declares Himself to be "compassionate and gracious...abounding in lovingkindness and truth" (Exodus 34:6).

- His lovingkindness and favor are everlasting because His nature is good and holy—and He never changes (1 Chronicles 16:34).

- In the Shepherd's Psalm, David wrote about his perspective of God's attitude toward him. He said, "Surely goodness and lovingkindness will follow me all the days of my life" (Psalm 23:6). Can you see how David was freed from fear as he recognized the permanent nature of God's goodness to him? Do you believe that goodness and lovingkindness are destined to follow you...no matter what?

- Rather than seeing the earth as being fraught with danger and peril, the psalmist wrote that the earth is "full of the lovingkindness of the Lord" (Psalm 33:5).

- In fact, the earth couldn't contain all the grace, favor, and love that God has; it "extends to the heavens"! (Psalm 36:5; see also 103:11).

- God's favor isn't an impersonal force. David needed the Lord's favor in a personal way when he was fleeing for his life from Saul. It was this favor that proved God wasn't just sitting idly by while His child was in need. No, David discovered that God was his stronghold and strength; in fact, he had seen His lovingkindness. Because of this he sang praises (Psalm 59:17).

- God's lovingkindness isn't just for "spiritual" people like David or Paul. It is abundantly flowing to *all* who call" upon God (Psalm 86:5). Why not call upon Him now? Ask Him to help you see how His lovingkindness is flowing to you today.

- Finally, let's look at Psalm 103. This psalm encourages us to remember all God's benefits. What do they consist of? God pardons all your iniquities, heals all your diseases, redeems your life from the pit, crowns you with lovingkindness and compassion! Andrea didn't know what it was like to be crowned with God's lovingkindness and compassion. Instead she felt a continual cloud of self-loathing, unbelief, and fear. Imagine the joy that could be ours if we really believed that His lovingkindness and compassion rested on us!

God's lovingkindness includes His grace, strength, and steadfast love. God's covenant with His children is one in which He promises to protect, pardon, and be merciful. In the same way that a strong loving father shelters, protects, and cares for a little child, our Father has promised to be gracious to us. If you're His child, He's granted you His favor and *nothing* will ever change that. In fact, when the apostle John describes the Messiah, he writes that He is "full of grace and truth" and that in Him we have received a fullness described as "grace upon grace" (John 1:14)—oceans of grace, one wave flowing over another.

In the movie *A Perfect Storm*, there was that one last monster wave that overcame the fishing crew of the *Andrea Gail*. Even as they fought their way up that wave, it was obvious that they weren't going to make it. The wave was just too strong. It overwhelmed their little vessel and flooded it with water. That's how God's grace is. It's overwhelming, it's inescapable, it's greater than you could ever imagine. The heavens and earth can't contain it and nothing you can do can stop it. But rather than drown us, His grace overwhelmingly sustains us—far more than we'll ever realize. Isn't that wonderful?

How God's Grace Changes Us

Grace to Be Holy

What does this overwhelming good will toward us mean? Does it mean that we can live any way that we like and flaunt our freedom and disregard His love? As Paul says, "May it never be!" (Romans 6:2). Part of God's grace is that we learn to live holy lives. In fact, grace teaches us to do just that. Titus 2:11-12 says,

> The grace of God has appeared, bringing salvation to all men, instructing us to deny ungodliness and worldly desires and to live sensibly, righteously and godly in the present age.

God loves us too much to allow us to continue in the joy-defeating sin that seems so inviting. As a perfect Father, He knows where our true happiness lies: Our old lives are dead and we've been made anew in Christ. Our new hearts will no longer find satisfaction in the tawdry baubles of this earth. We've been made citizens of heaven and it's only heaven's joys that will satisfy us. So God, by His grace, teaches us to deny ourselves those desires that we once loved.

Grace inclines our hearts to live lives that are sober and moderate. That doesn't mean that we don't enjoy the gifts God has given us in the world. It just means that we aren't "in love" with them—we use them moderately, recognizing them for what they are: transitory joys. His grace bends our hearts toward righteousness. Whereas we once relished the thought of coddling our pet sin, we are now learning, by His grace, to hate it and to love righteousness. It's the loving of righteous ways of thinking and acting that produces a godly lifestyle, and the love of true goodness is produced only by God's grace. So you see, a true measure of God's grace in one's life isn't careless living; rather, it's a life bent toward holiness. And a correct understanding of His grace realizes that we'll never be perfectly holy while here on earth. We'll never rely on holiness to earn anything from God, or trust in personal holiness to earn God's blessings. Instead, we can simply rejoice in God's faithful work in our lives—a work He chooses to do because He loves us. And grace teaches us to love what He loves, to fear what He commands us to fear, and to rest in Him.

Grace to Be Confident

What does the reality of God's grace mean to us? Does it mean that we'll never face tragedy, trouble, or difficulty? No, God never promises us that. What He does promise us—what is part of His gracious attitude toward us—is that we'll never suffer more difficulty than is necessary for His love to be known and enjoyed by us. That's the purpose of trials: to free us from our ties to the earth.

Because of God's sovereign rule in our lives, we can live confidently even when we're facing tragedy. Grace teaches us that tragedy and difficulty are no longer to be feared. The God who is strong enough to love us no matter what is also strong enough to control our circumstances. When He allows, for our good and His glory, something that appears to be a grave hardship or trouble, we can rest confidently in the truth that He may not be disciplining us and that even if He is, His love for us hasn't been diminished.

Examine, if you will, the focus of your fears. Do you fear illness, heartache, or trouble? Do you fear that you'll be unable to handle an unknown difficulty that might be headed your way? Do you believe that you have to work to be in God's "good graces"? The Lord is calling you to rest and confidently trust today. You can rest knowing that no matter how God has determined to weave the pattern of your life, even if that pattern is composed of some "dark threads," ultimately the design will be one of great beauty and bring you great joy. Even though Paul faced a weakness that plagued him (so much so that he prayed three times to be delivered), he knew the truth of God's grace. "My grace is sufficient for you," the Lord told him, "for power is perfected in weakness" (2 Corinthians 12:9). Paul knew the power of God's grace, which enabled him to live confidently and joyfully in the midst of a trial and personal weakness. And as a child of God, you can know the power of His grace, too.

Grace to Be Thankful

What is the purpose of God's graciousness toward us? That He would be praised and glorified! Of course, His grace results in our holiness, joy, and freedom from fear, but that joy is not to remain unspoken. Paul's encouragement to the Christians at Corinth was that the "grace which is spreading to more and more people may cause the giving of thanks to abound to the glory of God" (2 Corinthians 4:15). Do you see how a clear picture of God's grace would change Gloria, Louise, and Andrea's very lives? That's exactly what happened. As they came to understand God's grace, they no longer were filled with fear, worries, and anxieties. Their lives became marked by hearts overflowing with praise.

On her way to work, after spending time in humble prayer and joy-filled praise for God's promised goodness, Gloria would sing about and celebrate God's grace. No longer consumed with her own performance, she was able to consider Christ's performance and rest in it. She found that she was no longer tied to fears about accidents—in fact, on some mornings she was almost oblivious to the drive to work because she was having such a blessed time singing and worshiping Him.

Louise came to recognize God's sovereign rule over the universe and realized that her words and thoughts were not like God's: Her words didn't create reality. Because of God's grace, Louise learned that she could rest in His sovereign will and that

His will was *always* good. Although that will might mean times of great trial, she rejoiced in the knowledge that these trials came to her from a God whose unchanging disposition to her was one of grace. Her circumstances were not beyond what she could endure. Because she was not entrapped by continuous introspection, she was able to praise God for His power. Louise learned that God's grace would be sufficient for her, no matter what she faced.

Andrea developed a new habit upon awakening each morning. Instead of looking first at her own shortcomings, she purposely focused on Christ's perfections. On the nightstand by her bed she had note cards with Bible verses that she would read *before* she looked at her own shortcomings. She found that because she was no longer relying on her own self-righteousness, the Spirit was revealing sin to her that was deeper than she had ever seen before. For instance, she discovered that her gossip was more than just wrong words; it evidenced a heart that was proud and fearful. She didn't turn in terror from these realizations as she once had; now she humbly confessed them. *Yes, it's true that my sin is deep,* she would pray, *but your grace is deeper than my sin.* Once she confessed these sins she went on to thank God for His forgiveness and Christ's perfect record. Because she no longer felt the desire to spend her day proving her own righteousness, she was more able to confess her shortcomings to others, and her heart began to overflow with praise for God's great love.

A Grace That Perseveres

One of the joys of being a grandmother is getting to revisit my beloved children's books again. One of my favorites is *The Runaway Bunny* by Margaret Wise Brown.[4] In this precious story a little bunny tells his mother he is going to run away. The mother replied, "If you run away, I will run after you. For you are my little bunny." Then the bunny said he would become a fish and swim away. His mother said, "If you become a fish...I will become a fisherman and I will fish for you." The story continues along those lines—whatever the little bunny says he will do, the mother says she will do something that proves her unwavering love for her child.

At the end of the story the little bunny realizes that he can't escape his mother's great love, so he decides that he might as well stay home have a carrot and be her little bunny. The story is a great illustration of the strength and purpose of God's grace. In fact, it reminds me of Psalm 139, where God affirms His great love for us. As you meditate on these words, pray that God would enlighten your heart to His inescapable grace:

> "Where can I go from Your Spirit? Or where can I flee from Your presence? If I ascend to heaven, You are there; if I make my bed in Sheol, behold, You are there. If I take the wings of the dawn, if I dwell in the remotest part of the sea, even there Your hand will lead me, and Your right hand will lay hold of me. If I say, "Surely the darkness will overwhelm me, and the light around me will be night," even the darkness is not dark to You, and the night is as bright as the day. Darkness and light are alike to You."
>
> —Psalm 139:7-12

Resting in God's Grace

As I am seated here writing at my desk, I'm looking out over my lawn at the lovely tree in my front yard. The sky is blue and I can see the foothills in the distance clearly. There's no fog today. And as I've spent time meditating on God's grace again, I see Him a little more clearly, too. I'm remembering His great kindness and strong love—a love that refuses to let me go or fail to bless me. It's a love that I can rely on, a love that calms all my fears.

You, too, can experience the grace that overwhelms the soul, teaches you to desire holiness, and floods the heart so that it continually splashes over with praise. You don't need to worry or be fearful; in fact, all you have to do is rest. So, little one, why don't you curl up in your Father's love and enjoy Him? And from now on, whenever you see fog, remember to thank God for enabling you to see His character more clearly, so that you can rest in His promises and cease to be anxious about the things of life. And while you're thinking about it, why not have a nice carrot?

For Further Thought

1. The hymn "Amazing Grace" has been a blessing to Christians for many years. Take time now to sing through the words that you can remember and ponder how this grace can calm your fears.

2. I've listed here, for your benefit, a number of verses on grace. Write out each verse and its application to your life.

- Isaiah 38:17

- Romans 11:6

- Romans 12:6

- 1 Corinthians 15:10

- 2 Corinthians 6:1

- 2 Thessalonians 2:16-17

- 2 Timothy 2:1

3. The writer of Hebrews encouraged his readers to "draw near with confidence to the throne of grace, so that we may receive mercy and find grace to help in time of need" (Hebrews 4:16). How would seeing God's throne as a "throne of grace" change your attitude about prayer? Why would this writer encourage his readers to go to God to find mercy and grace in time of need? What do you need?

4. Jerry Bridges wrote, "Your worst days are never so bad that you are beyond the *reach* of God's grace. And your best days are never so good that you are beyond the *need* of God's grace. Every day of our Christian experience should be a day of relating to God on the basis of His grace alone."[5] Do you relate to God on the basis of His grace *alone* or do you act as if your daily relationship with Him is based on your works? How should your life change to reflect resting in His grace?

5. In the first column of the chart below, under the
   minus sign, list the sins you know you have committed recently. In the middle column, under the
   plus sign, note what has been done for you, out-
   weighing all your sins. With this in mind, use the
   third column to write Bible verses or write out a
   note of thanks for God's grace.

Your Sins (-)	The Perfections of Christ (+)	Praise for His Grace
1. 2. 3. 4. 5. 6. 7. 8. 9. 10.		*Father, I thank You that there is no sin that I could ever commit that could be greater than Your love...*

God's Strength Displayed in Your Weakness

"It is when we are conscious that we are feeble, and when we feel our need of aid, that the redeemer manifests His power to uphold, and imparts His purest consolations."[1]

—ALBERT BARNES
Nineteenth-century pastor and author

*A*s we have spent time together looking at our fears and how to overcome them, I trust that you've been blessed, strengthened, and encouraged. And before we begin this final chapter, let's take a moment to revisit the wonderful truths we've learned on our journey.

We began by looking at how God kindly gifted mankind with an ability to fear so that he would protect himself from danger. We also saw how that good gift was misused by our first parents in the Garden of Eden. They feared that perhaps God was withholding something from them, and they failed to fear what He had commanded: to not touch the tree of the knowledge of good and evil. As a result, they lost their innocence, their relationship with God, and life itself.

We saw how people throughout time, even the "heroes of faith" in the Bible, struggled with sinful fear. And we learned that because fear is such a formidable foe, we need to look outside of ourselves to the power of the Holy Spirit for victory and liberation. We need the Spirit's power to overcome the three primary causes of fear: the desire to control, the desire to please people, and the desire to be perfect. We also considered how disbelief in our heavenly Father's goodness, power, and wisdom plays a significant role in our fears.

Then we saw that without a firm belief in God's total control over all things, all hope of defeating fear is gone. We looked at the kind of fear that God has commanded—the fear of Him alone—and saw how that fear, coupled with love, can overcome all the nagging fearfulness that clamors for ascendence in our hearts. Then in the last chapter we looked at how a correct understanding of God's grace can help to alleviate our fears. Our fears usually have their roots in a misconception about God's character and His disposition toward His children.

In our final chapter together, I want to direct our focus to the concept of faith. We'll examine biblical faith and then we'll consider people in the Bible whose lives were memorialized for it. Remember, these aren't people who were fearless or superheroes. They struggled just like we do, and, by God's grace, their faith won out over their fear. The fear of God, love for Him and others, and faith in Christ are three potent fear-destroying weapons. And our goal in this chapter is to see how we can walk up the staircase of faith, from weak to strong faith, all in God's power.

Are You "Keeping the Faith"?

What is the state of your faith? If you're a Christian, I know you have faith in God, particularly the faith in Him that leads to salvation. But that's not the question I'm asking. I'm wondering what you depend on most in your day-to-day life. Do you primarily focus and depend on your feelings? Your fears? Your thoughts of what *might happen*? Where do you look for confidence as you face the challenges and trials of life? Who do you trust when the red light on the dashboard is blinking or the exit door of the store seems too far away?

Although faith is a foundational issue for Christians, it's one that many people are confused about even though *faith* is a word that we commonly use. You've probably heard people say, "I have faith in myself," or "If you believe in yourself, you can do anything." People generally use the words *belief* and *faith* interchangeably. But is that what the Bible talks about when it encourages us to have faith?

What is faith? The word that's commonly translated "faith" in the Bible means more than mere belief. It does mean belief, but it also implies dependence and trust. Faith, because it incorporates dependence and trust, also embodies action. This action can take many forms, as we'll see later when we look at Hebrews 11, but belief that doesn't eventuate in a changed life isn't true biblical faith. I'm not saying that faith can't be weak at times or that it doesn't struggle. But I am saying that it's *living...it moves...it can be perceived*. That's because faith that is true faith trusts and depends on God.

Trust Me—I'll Catch You!

Living in Southern California, it was imperative that our children learn to swim at an early age. At four years old, our eldest son James was afraid of the water, and we had to work for days to get him to "take the plunge." My husband would stand in the water at the edge of the pool and call to James to jump to him. When James hesitated, we would ask him if he believed that we would catch him. "Yes," he said, "I believe that you'll catch me," but his feet were still dry and rooted to the edge of the pool. "Then jump," we would reply. We could tell that he wanted to jump, he wanted to trust us, but his fears were stronger than his faith. We knew that James had progressed from simply *saying that he believed* to *actual faith* when he leapt into his father's arms at the edge of the pool. Of course, once we got him going, there was no stopping him...and now he lives near the beach and surfs as often as his schedule will allow.

Do you see the difference between belief and faith? James *knew* that his dad was standing there, waiting with his arms outstretched. He *mentally assented* to the truth that his dad would catch him. But the pool looked big and frightening and he wasn't sure that he could *trust*. And that's what makes the difference between belief and faith. Faith is more than a simple acknowledgment of a fact: it's a firm persuasion or conviction. And it *always* eventuates in action. Perhaps this action isn't as obvious as leaping off the edge of the pool; perhaps it's as unrecognizable as a prayer in the heart or the decision to take one step out of the house. Faith doesn't have to be flamboyant, but it does have life.

People Remembered for Their Faith

Let's look at the one chapter in the Bible that's entirely devoted to shining the spotlight on people of faith. The chapter is Hebrews 11, and below I've summarized what the Holy Spirit has written about some of these people. But before you read on, let me encourage you to stop and read through Hebrews 11 for yourself.

Now, starting with verse 4, let's look at the people who serve as examples of faith:

- Verse 4 highlights Abel, Adam and Eve's son, who offered to God an acceptable sacrifice. By this action, done in faith, God declared him to be righteous, and "though he is dead, he still speaks." What does he say? How do we know that he had a faith that pleased God? His faith was observable, wasn't it? Although he was killed by his brother for his faithful obedience, his life is a testimony to us today. It tells us to obey God in the face of opposition and fear of displeasing others.

- Enoch was an Old Testament saint whom God took directly to heaven; thus Enoch never faced death. This man of faith is known as one who "pleased God." God chose to keep Enoch from the trial of death because his faith pleased Him. In what way did Enoch please God? By having faith that God existed and that He rewarded those who sought after Him. We don't know exactly what Enoch did to demonstrate his faith, but we do know that he was rewarded by God for his faith. Enoch knew that "without faith it [was] impossible to please Him"[2] (verse 6), but he also believed that God would reward his faith when he sought after Him. Do you believe that God will reward you as you seek, in faith, to please Him? Faith encompasses not only belief in God's existence, but belief also in His intimate participation in His children's lives. It is this kind of faith that is always rewarded. It may not be rewarded for you in the same way that it is for others, but it is always rewarded nevertheless.

- You know the story of Noah, and how he prepared an ark for the salvation of his family when God's just judgment was coming. He was "warned about things not yet seen" so in "*holy fear* built an ark" (verse 7 NIV, emphasis added) and became an "heir of the righteousness that comes by faith." Sometimes acting in faith seems foolish. Other times it means working hard sawing wood and pounding nails. Again, your faith is demonstrated by the righteous acts you perform even though you might be shaking in your boots as you speak to a neighbor about Christ, run errands for your family, or contribute to the church's mission fund. It's at these times that the fear of God must overcome all other fears.

- We looked at Abraham and Sarah in chapter 2 of this book. Abraham first demonstrated his faith by leaving his home and following God's call, "not knowing where he was going" (verse 8). Can you imagine the fears that must have plagued both him and Sarah? How would you feel if your spouse came home today and told you that God had instructed him to pack up and move to an unknown destination? Would you be afraid? Worried? Verses 15-16 tell us why Abraham and Sarah were able to obey this difficult command: they were longing for a heavenly home.

What are you longing for? If you long for earthly security or pleasure, then fear will win over faith. If your riches are here on earth, then they are subject to destruction or loss, and that possibility will make you fearful. But if your treasure really is in heaven, you'll be able to act in faith because you don't have anything to lose. On the contrary, you'll have peace, knowing that your heavenly treasure is safe under God's protective care.

- When Moses was born, the faith of his parents, Amram and Jochebed, gave them the courage to disobey the king's command that he be killed. In fact, verse 23 says, "they were not afraid of the king's edict." Do you think that means there wasn't any trepidation in their hearts about what Pharaoh might do? Or might it possibly mean that in comparison to their faith, the fear meant nothing? What was the faith that they had? That somehow, in some way, God would protect their baby and use him for His glory.

Sometimes faith means going against the prevailing wisdom or taking risks. At other times it means we will face difficult circumstances we don't understand at all and the only option we have is to hang on and put our complete trust in God. In some cases, God responds like He did with Moses and saves lives. At other times a martyr's death awaits, but there is one thing you can be sure of: at all times, God rewards faith, and whatever the outcome, He'll use it for your ultimate good and His glory. Can you imagine how faith mingled with the timid concern that was in the heart of Moses' sister Miriam as she watched the little basket float downstream? *I know God will help my baby brother....Oh, Lord, please help him.* What little basket do you need to float downstream in faith and trust that God will protect and use it? Don't think that your faith has to be free from any concerns before you exercise it. Just let go and trust Him—and see what He will do.

- Can you imagine the fear the Israelites felt as they heard Joshua's plan to take over Jericho? March around the city silently, for six days, and then shout. These people were a whole new generation—they had heard about how God had divided the Red Sea 40 years earlier, but none of them had actually seen God's ability to defeat a strong enemy (except Joshua and Caleb). Don't let your familiarity with the story rob you of the wonder of it. In simple trust they marched around a strongly fortified city and then expected the walls to fall down. Wouldn't you be afraid? I know I would. Do you have faith God can bring down the well-fortified walls of fear, worry, doubt, and anxiety in your heart? God's command to trust Him and act upon His Word might seem as useless to you as the marching might have seemed to the Israelites. Think for a moment: These were not people who were known for their great faith. But, in this one case, they had the grace to trust and obey. Will you obey in whatever God is calling you to do? Do you believe He will catch you if you jump? Do you really trust Him?

Hebrews 11 closes by summarizing the works of faith performed by others. They "conquered kingdoms, performed acts of righteousness, obtained promises, shut the mouths of lions, quenched the power of fire, escaped the edge of the sword, *from weakness were made strong*, became mighty in war, put foreign armies to flight" (verses 33-34, emphasis added). These "heroes of faith" weren't always strong. No, the Bible says that "from weakness [they] were made strong." Do you feel weak? Do you think you'll never be able to change? Then you're just the sort of person that God loves to transform. In fact, it's that weakness itself that will work for you, teaching you to put your trust in Him, to have faith. And as you grow in faith, you'll find that you're one of the people in whom the Lord will prove Himself most strong.

Today, if you feel weak and unable to obey, then thank Him. Thank Him that you're not able to be so foolish as to trust in yourself or rely on your own strength. Thank Him that the strength will have to come from Him because you don't have any strength of your own. Then rise up and start walking around that city, build that ark, send your dearest desire down the river into God's keeping...and let Him do what He knows is best to do. When it comes to life's challenges, I'd much rather put them into God's all-sovereign hands than frail human hands, wouldn't you?

A Definition of Faith

So, what is faith? *It is the knowledge of God's character, the belief that He's able to do all that He's promised, and the trust to follow Him wherever He leads.* For you, that might mean standing before the church singing in the choir, facing the reality that you might forget your lines or seem foolish. It might mean that you'll have to care for a sick person even though you feel overwhelmed by the prospect of doing so. Perhaps your concern has to do with driving your car on the freeway or going shopping for the family. Acting in faith may even mean that you'll have to endure real feelings of panic so that you can love your neighbor the way that God calls you to. In these—and millions of other ways—you can live out your faith, and God will reward you. He might not reward you with the immediate loss of the symptoms of your fear, but as you focus on Christ-honoring obedience, you'll find that your symptoms of fear don't mean quite so much to you anymore. And, in time, Lord willing, you'll find that they don't matter at all. Eventually you'll come to notice that you haven't experienced the symptoms for a while. No matter how weak you are, you can be made strong in Him.

Faith's Muscle Builders

I'm sure you're wondering how you can have more faith. Let me direct you to some practical steps you can take to strengthen your faith and become a victor over your fear.

To help you remember these steps, I've drawn a staircase that, with each step, progresses from weakness to strength. I've also used the word *faith* as an acronym in the chart.

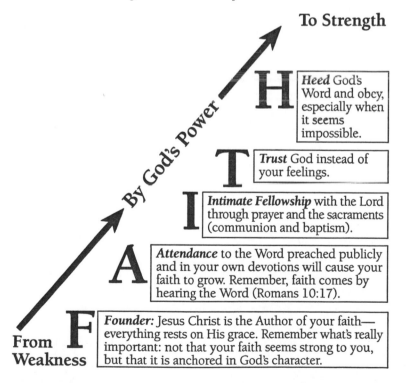

To Strength

By God's Power

Heed God's Word and obey, especially when it seems impossible.

Trust God instead of your feelings.

Intimate Fellowship with the Lord through prayer and the sacraments (communion and baptism).

Attendance to the Word preached publicly and in your own devotions will cause your faith to grow. Remember, faith comes by hearing the Word (Romans 10:17).

From Weakness

Founder: Jesus Christ is the Author of your faith—everything rests on His grace. Remember what's really important: not that your faith seems strong to you, but that it is anchored in God's character.

Remember how the people in Hebrews 11 were described? They were people whose faith had been transformed *from weakness to strength*. And because God doesn't play favorites, He can do the same for you. You're probably not in the same circumstances as those in Hebrews 11, but you can trust that God will reward your steps of faith with stronger faith and freedom from fear. Let's take a closer look at each step on our staircase from weakness to strength.

Founder—Interestingly, the first step has nothing to do with you. The first step is the one that God takes when He plants within your heart the faith that He alone authors. Hebrews 12:2 tells us that it is Jesus who is the Author and Perfecter of our faith. He begins it, He sustains it, He causes it to grow according to His sovereign plan. He is the Founder, and it's only because of His grace that He's given it to you.

Attendance to the Word. The apostle Paul wrote that faith grows by hearing the Word of God: "Faith comes from hearing, and hearing by the word of Christ" (Romans 10:17). Peter echoed this thought as he enjoined his reader to "long for the pure milk of the word, so that by it *you may grow* in respect to salvation" (1 Peter 2:2, emphasis added).

Attendance to God's Word has at least two aspects. First, there is attendance to the Word preached. I don't think I can overemphasize the importance of feeding frequently on God's Word in the context of a church service. It is vital that you are in a church that preaches the Word faithfully, clearly, and correctly. You should find that the preaching both consoles and challenges you—or, as the Puritans used to say, "Good preaching should comfort the distressed and distress the comfortable." Just as bodies grow strong because of good nutrition, faith most commonly grows in response to hearty feasting on regular servings of God's truth, applied directly to the heart by the Holy Spirit. Nibbling on chocolate éclairs might be pleasurable for a little while, but if you make a steady diet of it, you'll eventually become weak and sickly. If you aren't in a solid, Bible-preaching church, then the absolute first step you need to take is to get into one. Don't settle for anything less.

If you have trouble getting out of the house, begin by listening to tapes of sermons, with the goal of eventually attending a church. Perhaps you could arrange for someone to drive you there for the first few times. In any case, remember that God will reward even the faltering steps that you take as you seek to obey Him in faith.

Attendance to the Word of God also has a second facet: personal Bible study. This study can take many forms, but it needs to be both consistent and relevant to your life. If you're unfamiliar with the idea of studying the Bible, let me recommend that you begin by reading the Gospel of John. With pen and paper in hand, read one chapter each day. Ask God to illuminate your heart to the truth about Christ (remember, it's the Word that builds your faith). For each portion of the Scripture that you read, ask yourself the following questions:

1. What is the meaning of this passage?

2. Why did the Holy Spirit include it?

3. How can I take the truth that I've read and apply it in my life today?

If you get stuck on a passage you can't understand, then move on to the next passage. If you'd like help with understanding difficult Bible verses, look them up in a good Bible commentary, such as *Barnes' Notes on the New Testament,* Kregel Publications; *Adam Clarke's Commentary on the Bible,* World Publishing Co; *Matthew Henry's Commentary on the Whole Bible,* Hedrickson Publishers, Inc. There are also helpful Bible studies that have been written by godly men and women. Inquire at a Christian bookstore for one that they would recommend.

Consider your time in the Scriptures to be a spiritual meal. You'll receive nourishment from the Word that will help to strengthen your faith. Remember that it isn't enough to read Christian fiction novels or even biographies (although they may be beneficial). It's the *Word of God alone* that God has promised to use to help you grow, and it's the Word that you need to feed upon on a daily basis.

Intimate fellowship through prayer and sacraments (communion and baptism) is the next important step on the staircase of faith.

Some Christians mistakenly assume their prayers must be of a certain length or extraordinarily eloquent for God to be pleased. Instead, God wants us to speak to Him as "familiarly as a son speaks to an earthly father."[4] Rather than think that you must impress God with your words, look at prayer as a pouring out of your heart before your Father. Speak to Him without reserve about your fears and concerns. Confess any sin of unbelief or disobedience, and thank Him for His forgiveness. Request from Him the understanding and strength that you need in order to follow Him faithfully that day. It is when you've opened your heart to Him for His observance that your "cares are…greatly lightened, and your confidence of obtaining your requests increases."[5] Prayer will strengthen your faith because you'll have the confidence that He hears you and that you've done what He's asked of you by praying. John wrote of this confidence, saying, "This is the confidence which we have before Him, that, if we ask anything according to His will, He hears us. And if we know that He hears us in whatever we ask, we know that we have the requests which we have asked from Him" (1 John 5:14-15).

Another less-recognized avenue for building your faith is by partaking of the sacraments: communion and baptism. Because it isn't within the scope of this book to write extensively on these blessed institutions, may I just briefly direct your thinking?

We know that communion builds our faith because when we partake of it, we are remembering the Lord's death—His sacrifice for sin. In doing so, we are preaching the gospel to ourselves again: watching the bread being broken, looking into the cup of blessing. These things remind us of that wonderfully terrifying good news: Christ died for sinners; Christ died for me! And not only that, but He is ruling and reigning even now, and Scripture encourages us to anticipate His quick return. Fight the tendency to look at communion as common or ordinary; watch the breaking of the bread and the passing out of the elements with great care. Observe the oneness that you have with the Lord and with His body, the church. Let communion preach faith to your heart.

Baptism strengthens your faith for the same reasons. Baptism represents, in part, the death, burial, and resurrection of the Lord, and in observing it first, in your own life, and secondly in others, you are reminded anew of that glorious news: Jesus Christ died to save sinners! We, who are His, have entered into His death and resurrection, and we are now able to walk in newness of life! (Romans 6:1).[6]

So, when it's time for a baptism or communion service at your church, attend to these ordinances with great diligence, being careful to watch in faith, asking God to quicken your understanding to the spiritual truth revealed by the natural elements of bread, wine, and water.

By the way, attendance to the Word, prayer, communion, and baptism are not meritorious in themselves. In other words, they don't make God love you more than He already does. They are simply the outward *means* or *avenues of grace* that God normally uses to strengthen the faith He's placed in your heart.

Trust God instead of your feelings. It's so easy to have faith in our emotions, isn't it? I know that it's a continual struggle for me to tell myself that just because I *feel* a certain way doesn't mean it's the truth. If you're one who suffers from panic attacks, you'll find this the most difficult step to take. Let me encourage you by saying that you won't actually faint, your heart won't pound so hard that it explodes in your chest, and you won't go crazy. It's during those times that you'll have to remember that God is greater than your feelings and has promised to reward your faith. These first steps will seem so hard—everything in you will be telling you to stop, to protect yourself, to disbelieve. But the Holy Spirit will be there with you, encouraging you to walk by faith, and not by what you see or feel (2 Corinthians 5:7). Faith, by its nature, flies in the face of what you can observe with your natural eyes or feel with your emotions. Faith isn't faith if it rests upon temporal braces such as sight and feelings. As 2 Corinthians 4:18 says, "the things which are seen are temporal, but the things which are not seen are eternal."

Remember, you serve the sovereign King who is also your loving heavenly Father. He will protect, encourage, and reward you as you seek to obey Him in faith, no matter what your pounding heart is telling you.

Heed and obey God's Word, especially when it seems impossible to do so. Faithful obedience breeds greater faith and obedience, one step leading spontaneously to the next. At times faith-filled obedience seems like the exact opposite of what we should do. Look again at the lives of those listed in Hebrews 11. The obedience that their faith generated seemed to fly in the face of reason, and their hearts must have been filled with fear. But, they saw the choices differently. They saw life through the eyes of faith and knew that, as Charles Spurgeon said, "Our greatest risk is over when we obey."[7]

Do you see that what you should fear most is disobedience? Do you fear displeasing the Father who so loves you and who has every right to command you? He has this right because He is your Creator and your Redeemer. Every command that He places upon you is for your ultimate happiness and His glory. Don't despair! Even a very weak faith is strong because, if it is true faith, it's tied to the one who has all power in heaven and earth. Your focus should not be on the greatness of your faith, but rather on the greatness of the one in whom you trust. Your faith may be weak, but because of His majesty, it can accomplish much. God is strong enough to hold on to you, to keep you, and to enable you to obey, even when it seems most difficult. It's by His strong grace that you'll be able to grow in obedience and faith and come to know the diminishing of your fears. As Spurgeon said, "When our only care is to obey, a thousand other cares take the flight."[8]

From Weakness Made Strong

You can become one about whom it is said, "From weakness, you've been made strong." You can count on the veracity of that truth because the ground that the promise rests on isn't your strength, fearlessness, or faith. Rather, the promise rests on the greatness of your omnipotent King, and He isn't worried about your weakness. In fact, He delights in your dependence and trust. It's His special pleasure to take the weak and make them strong because it's in that way that He is most glorified.

Let me remind you of what I said in the introduction to this book: "What I've written here is not offered as the answer to all your problems, but it will point you to the one who is." It's my prayer that through these pages and by God's grace, you have become more aware of His kindness and life-changing power. Perhaps when you began this book you weren't aware of the depth of your struggle with fear. Or, perhaps like so many others, you were more than aware of your struggle, but didn't really understand your fear's origins. As you have seen both the source and magnitude of your battle, I trust that you have also come to know and trust the one who both knows your fear intimately and has the power to triumph over it. He is the Life-Changer, and it's in Him alone that you'll find the grace you need.

A Thousand Fears Taking Flight

Frequently during spring and summer afternoons, I like to sit out on my back patio. At about six o'clock each evening there is a flock of blackbirds that fly over en route to their evening rest. The number of birds is astonishing—hundreds, at least—and when I'm sitting with little Wesley, we both cheer and laugh while they go squawking overhead. The family has joked about Alfred Hitchcock's hair-raising movie *The Birds* and what we would do if these birds decided to land on our patio. But they've never done that, and we really enjoy watching them fly over and screaming, "Birdies, birdies!"

Think, if you will, about your fears. Can you name them? Do you understand how they function? More importantly, do you know who can cause them to "take flight"? The Lord Jesus Christ has faced every fear and has done so on your behalf. It's because of His triumph over fear that you can grow toward true freedom. In fact, Hebrews 2:14-15 affirms the truth that one reason He came was to free you from fear:

> Therefore, since the children share in flesh and blood, He Himself likewise also partook of the same, that through death He might render powerless him who had the power of death, that is, the devil, *and might free those who through fear of death were subject to slavery all their lives* (emphasis added).

Because of what Christ has done—setting free we who were once slaves of fear—you can watch you fears fly away, like the blackbirds, knowing that they've been vanquished by the one who alone has the power to dispel them. It's not your goodness, your power, your understanding, or even your great faith that will send them on their way. It's Him alone—so let me encourage you again with just one final word from our friend, Charles Spurgeon:

I have no cares, O blessed Lord,
For all my cares are Thine;
I live in triumph, too, for Thou
Hast made Thy triumphs mine.[9]

Your cares are His and His triumphs are yours, so now you can boldly say, "The Lord is my helper, I will not be afraid" (Hebrews 13:6).

For Further Study

1. What is the difference between belief and faith? What is the evidence of faith?

2. In Ephesians 1:17-19, Paul prayed that God would grant certain graces to his readers. What were they? How would having these graces cause your faith to grow?

3. In Mark 9:17-24, read the story of the father of a demon-possessed boy. Think about the emotions this grief-stricken father was experiencing. What was Jesus' answer to his weak faith?

4. Why is the seeming weakness or strength of your faith not that significant?

5. Outline the steps for growing in faith as explained by the staircase illustration on page 203.

6. First John 5:4-5 speaks of our faith overcoming the world. What does this phrase mean? What is the relationship between verses 4 and 5?

7. Take time now to think about what you've learned in these pages and summarize your thoughts here in a prayer of trust and thanksgiving:

A

How You Can Know
if You Are a Christian

I'm so glad that you decided to turn to this page, way in the back of this book—and there are two reasons I feel this way.

First of all, the truths that are contained in this book will be impossible for you to understand and follow if you aren't a Christian, and I want you to be able to know the joy of God-empowered change. But, that really isn't the most important reason I'm glad that you decided to turn here.

I'm also pleased you turned to this page because God longs for you to know the joy of peace with Him and to have the assurance that your sins are forgiven. You see, if you've never really come to the place in your life where you have acknowledged the truth of God's great love and sacrifice and your need for forgiveness, you must question whether you really are a Christian.

Many people attend church or try to live "good" lives. We certainly aren't as bad as we could be (we think)...and so, like Patrick Swayze in *Ghost,* we think it doesn't really matter if we have placed our trust in Christ. After all, if we're nice and we love people, God will accept us...right? If the decision were up to me or someone else, we would probably say that we're all okay. But, that's not the truth, and the decision isn't up to me or another person. It's up to God—and His standards are different than ours. He says, "My ways are not your ways and My thoughts are not your thoughts" (see Isaiah 55:8).

The truth is that God is perfectly holy. That means that He never thinks or does anything that is inconsistent with His perfection. He is pure and without fault of any kind. That's not because He gets up every morning and says, "I'll try to be good today." No, by His nature He is good and there is never a time when He isn't.

In addition to being perfectly holy, God is just. That means that He always sees that justice is served, or those who deserve punishment will always receive it in the end. Now, I know that it may not seem that way to you, looking at things like we do from an earthly perspective, but let me assure you, the Great Judge of all the earth will prevail. If God allowed people to get away with breaking His laws, then He wouldn't really be holy, would He?

In one sense, the truth of God's holiness and justice reassures us. The Hitlers of the world, even though they seem to have escaped judgment here on earth, will stand before their Creator and will receive exactly what they deserve. But, in another sense, God's holiness and justice should make us all uncomfortable. That's because even though we may not be as bad as we could be, we know that we all sin, and God hates sin. Very simply speaking, *sin is any violation of God's perfect standards*. His standards are contained in the Bible and were summed up in the Ten Commandments in the Old Testament. Think for a moment about those commandments: Have you had any other gods in your life? Have you reverenced the Lord's day and set it apart for Him? Have you always honored those in authority over you? Have you ever taken another's life or turned your back on someone who needed your protection? Have you ever desired someone who was not your spouse? Have you ever taken anything that wasn't yours to take? Have you ever told a lie or looked at something that someone else had and wanted it for yourself?

I'm sure, if you're like me, you'll say that you've probably broken a number of God's commands at various times in your life. And there's no way you can avoid the time when one day, you will stand before God's judgment seat. And the Bible makes it clear that the wages of sin is death (see Romans 6:23). That's the punishment that sin deserves. But don't despair: If you know that you are a sinner, then there is hope for you because God is not only holy and just, He is also merciful.

God has immense love and mercy and because of this, He made a way for you and me to come to Him. He did this without compromising His holiness and justice. You see, someone had to take the punishment for your sin. Someone had to die in your place. But, who could do this and still maintain God's justice?

Every person that has ever lived has sinned and was therefore disqualified from taking someone else's punishment because they deserved punishment of their own. Only one Man could take this punishment. Only one Man was perfectly sinless and completely undeserving of punishment. That Man was Jesus Christ. Jesus was both God (making Him perfectly sinless) and man (making Him suitable as our "stand-in"). The Bible teaches that because of God's love for man, He sent His Son, Jesus Christ, to die in our place. On the cross, Jesus took the punishment we deserved. Thus is God's justice served and His holiness upheld. That's why the Bible teaches that "while we were yet sinners, Christ died for us" (Romans 5:8).

But that still leaves you with a problem. Perhaps as you are reading this you know that you are a sinner. You also know that God is holy and just, and you are hoping that He is as merciful and loving as I've portrayed Him. What must you do? You must believe on Him. That means that you must believe what the Bible says about God, you, and your sin, and you must ask God to forgive you of all your sins. You can do this through prayer. There aren't any special words that you must say. In fact, the Bible says that "everyone who calls on the name of the Lord will be saved" (Acts 2:21). You can pray to Him, asking Him to forgive your sin because of Jesus' sacrifice. You

can ask Him to make you His own. The Bible says, "If we confess our sins, He is faithful and righteous to forgive us our sins
and to cleanse us from all unrighteousness" (1 John 1:9). You
can rest in His truthfulness.

Now, if you have become a Christian, you will want to live
for Him in a way that pleases Him. In order to know how to
do that, you must begin reading His Word. You should begin
in the Gospel of John with the first chapter. As you read, pray
that God will help you to understand.

The next thing that you should do is find a good Bible-
believing church and start attending it. A Bible-believing
church is one that believes in the Trinity (that the Father, the
Son, and the Holy Spirit are equally one God), believes that salvation is entirely a free gift of God, practices prayer and holiness, and preaches from God's Word (without any other books
added).

If you've become a Christian through the ministry of this
book, I would love to know so that I can rejoice with you.
Please write to me through the publisher: Harvest House Publishers, 990 Owen Loop North, Eugene, OR, 97402.

May God's richest blessings be yours as you bow humbly
before His throne!

APPENDIX

B

Filtering Your Thoughts

Thought Filters:	Ask Yourself:
True	Is what I'm thinking *true* about God, particularly His fatherly care for me?
Honorable	Do my thoughts honor God? Do they reflect the knowledge that He is wonderful, kind, loving, wise, and powerful?
Right	Are my thoughts holy, righteous, or just? Are they the kind that the Lord Himself would think?
Pure	Does my thought cast doubt on God's goodness or the truth of His promises? Does it elevate my own importance or desire?
Lovely	Do my thoughts flow from a heart filled with tenderness and affection for the LORD? Would my thoughts bring Him pleasure?
Of Good Repute	Are my thoughts of good repute? Are they grounded in faith?
Excellent	Do my thoughts cause me to be fearful, or do they fill my heart with courage and strong commitment to virtuous living?
Praiseworthy	Would the Lord commend my thoughts? Would they bring Him glory?

Day	Task (DV)	Time Needed	Benefit
Monday			
Tuesday			
Wednesday			
Thursday			
Friday			
Saturday			
Sunday			

NOTES

Chapter 1—Understanding How Fear Works
1. "Our Needless Fears," a sermon delivered on Thursday evening June 11, 1874 by C. H. Spurgeon at the Metropolitan Tabernacle, Newington (from *Spurgeon's Encyclopedia of Sermons* electronic database. Copyright © 1997 by Biblesoft).
2. Ibid.
3. Because I'm not a physician, I'd like to recommend that you get a good physical exam to rule out physical causes for your anxieties.
4. Some people believe that there are inborn traits or chemical imbalances at the bottom of these fears. At the time of this writing I haven't read anything that has convinced me. There are, of course, changes in brain chemistry in the habitually fearful person. But what still hasn't been proven is whether this abnormal brain chemistry is the *cause* or the *effect*. For more information see Elliot Valenstein, *Blaming the Brain: The Truth About Drugs and Mental Health* (New York: Free Press, 1998); Ed Welch, *Blame It on the Brain?: Distinguishing Chemical Imbalances, Brain Disorders, and Disobedience* (Phillipsburg, NJ: P & R Publishing, 1998); Sydney Walker, *A Dose of Sanity: Mind, Medicine and Misdiagnosis* (New York: John Wiley & Sons, 1997).
5. I first thought about panic attacks in this way after reading G. R. Fisher "Those Mysterious Panic Attacks" in *The Journal of Pastoral Practice*, vol. 6, no. 2, 1983, p. 35.

Chapter 2—Bible Heroes Who Struggled with Fear
1. Thomas Watson, *A Christian Directory* (Morgan, PA: Soli Deo Gloria Publications, 1996), p. 292. *A Christian Directory: A Sum of Practical Theology, and Cases of Conscience* was first published in 1654.
2. God stopped Abimelech from touching Sarah, "and I also kept you from sinning against Me; therefore I did not let you touch her" (Genesis 20:6).
3. C.S. Lewis, *The Lion, the Witch and the Wardrobe* in The Chronicles of Narnia (New York: Harper Collins Juvenile Books, 1994).

Chapter 3—Replacing Your Fear with God's Power
1. *Spurgeon's Encyclopedia of Sermons* electronic database. Copyright © 1997 by Biblesoft.
2. See also Romans 8:2; 2 Corinthians 3:17; 6:18; Ephesians 1:19; Colossians 1:29.
3. Corrie ten Boom, *The Hiding Place* (Grand Rapids: Chosen Books, 1971), p. 33.
4. *Spurgeon's Encyclopedia of Sermons* electronic database. Copyright © 1997 by Biblesoft.
5. Jerry Bridges, *Trusting God Even When Life Hurts* (Colorado Springs: NavPress, 1988), p. 18.
6. Philip Bennett Power, as quoted in Jerry Bridges, Ibid., p. 203.

Chapter 4—When You Feel You're Losing Control
1. See Exodus 3:15-17.
2. *Matthew Henry's Commentary on the Whole Bible*, New Modern Edition, electronic database. Copyright © 1991 by Hendrickson Publishers.
3. Ibid.

Chapter 5—Fearing the People Around Us

1. Edward T. Welch, *When People Are Big and God Is Small: Overcoming Peer Pressure, Codependency, and the Fear of Man* (Phillipsburg, NJ: P & R Publishing, 1997), p. 19. This wonderful book is a precious resource for anyone who struggles with the fear of man, which is euphemistically called "peer pressure," "codependency," and "shyness" in our culture.
2. *Matthew Henry's Commentary on the Whole Bible*, New Modern Edition, electronic database. Copyright © 1991 by Hendrickson Publishers, Inc.
3. Os Guiness, *The Call: Finding and Fulfilling the Central Purpose of Your Life* (Nashville: Word Publishing, 1998), p. 74.
4. *Barnes's Notes*, electronic database. Copyright © 1997 by Biblesoft.
5. Guiness, Ibid., p. 77.

Chapter 6—The Fear Caused by Perfectionism

1. In our struggle with perfectionism, our tendency may be to underplay God's standard. In trying to get free from what appears to be impossibly high standards of performance, we may be tempted to neglect Jesus' teaching on this topic. It is at this point that we must be careful that we don't lower or distort God's Word to fit our purposes, even if those purposes seem good.
2. Of course, there are some who believe that perfection this side of heaven is attainable. It seems to me that this belief can be held only if the standard is lowered to include only outward sins such as adultery, lying, or stealing, and not the inner, more hidden sins such as anger, lust, self-indulgence, or covetousness.
3. I.D.E. Thomas, *A Golden Treasury of Puritan Quotations* (Carlisle, PA: The Banner of Truth Trust, 1997), p. 207.
4. See also Isaiah 53:10-12; Daniel 9:24; 2 Corinthians 5:21; Ephesians 1:6; Philippians 3:9; Revelation 7:9-17.
5. Richard Baxter, *A Christian Directory* (Morgan, PA: Soli Deo Gloria Publications, 1996), p. 75.
6. Thanks to Paul Tripp for pointing out this verse and its application.

Chapter 7—God Really Does Care for You

1. *Matthew Henry's Commentary on the Whole Bible*, New Modern Edition, electronic database. Copyright ©1991 by Hendrickson Publishers, Inc., comment on Matthew 6:33.
2. Ralph C. Merkle, *Power of the Human Brain*, an internet article. This article first appeared in *Foresight Update*, No. 6, August 1989.
3. Paul said the same thing in 2 Corinthians 3:4-5, "Such confidence we have through Christ toward God. Not that we are adequate in ourselves to consider anything as coming from ourselves, but *our adequacy is from God....*"
4. Ric Ergenbright, *The Art of God: The Heavens and the Earth* (Wheaton, IL: Tyndale House Publishers, 1999).
5. Some teach that it is very difficult or perhaps even impossible to trust God as your heavenly Father if you haven't had a good earthly father. Although this argument seems logical at first blush, it is analogous to saying that I can't relate to God as my Master because I have a wicked employer or that I can't understand God's kingly rule because I've had poor examples as president. I'm not saying that our childhood relationships don't matter. What I am saying is that all of God's children can learn to

trust Him as Father because we're never to assign to God's character what we see in sinful man. If nothing else, our earthly fathers can stand as examples of what our heavenly Father is not.

6. Matthew Henry, ibid.
7. *Spurgeon's Encyclopedia of Sermons,* exposition of Matthew 6:5-34, electronic database. Copyright © 1997 by Biblesoft.
8. I'm not saying that it's sinful to make a sandwich or to cook for your guests. I'm asking you to question the primary focus of your life. We're commanded to practice hospitality and to eat properly so that we can maintain our health. It's just that even in the middle of spreading the mayonnaise or barbecuing the burgers, we need to be seeking His kingdom and our growth in holiness. After all, people won't remember five years from now whether or not the gravy was lumpy. What they will remember is whether they learned more about God and His love.

Chapter 8—The Security of God's Sovereignty
1. Arthur W. Pink, *The Sovereignty of God* (Grand Rapids: Baker Books, 1999), p. 34.
2. Jerry Bridges, *Trusting God Even When Life Hurts* (Colorado Springs: NavPress, 1988), p. 36.
3. As you look over this list, I'm sure that you have questions about man's free will and the devil's power. Let me just say that I believe that the Bible teaches that we do freely make responsible choices. God never forces anyone to love Him against his own will, nor does He cause anyone to sin. God commands all people to come to Him, and those who want to, do so (see Matthew 11:25-28). The question is not whether we're forced to come to Him or stopped when we want to come. The question is one of desire: all who want to come to Him, will.

Also, the devil is powerful, but can't do anything without God's permission, as the story of Job so vividly portrays. Satan is a created being, and like all created beings, is under the authority of the Creator.

I would recommend the following books on this topic: *Trusting God Even When Life Hurts* by Jerry Bridges (NavPress, 1988); *The Sovereignty of God* by Arthur W. Pink (Baker Books, 1999); *Chosen by God* by R.C. Sproul (Tyndale House, 1986).
4. Pink, ibid.
5. *Barnes's Notes,* by Albert Barnes, D.D., electronic database. Copyright © 1997 by Biblesoft.
6. Quoted in Pink, ibid., p. 191.
7. Doris Van Stone, *No Place to Cry: The Hurt and Healing of Sexual Abuse* (Chicago: Moody Press, 1990), p. 118.
8. The emperor did issue the death sentence, but Luther was protected and hidden for a year while the emperor became embroiled in other issues. During his forced seclusion, Luther translated the New Testament into German. God's sovereign hand protected Luther, yet at the same time restricted his movements so that he would have time to translate the Bible.
9. *Spurgeon's Encyclopedia of Sermons,* "An Instructive Truth—Jeremiah 10:23." A sermon delivered on Thursday evening, June 22, 1876 by C. H. Spurgeon at the Metropolitan Tabernacle, Newington. Electronic database. Copyright © 1997 by Biblesoft.

Chapter 9—The Fear That Results in Blessings

1. Jay E. Adams, *The Christian Counselor's New Testament*, (Hackettstown, SC: Timeless Texts, 1994), p. 224.
2. Ibid., p. 825.
3. Edward T. Welch, *When People Are Big and God Is Small* (Phillipsburg, NJ: P & R Publishing, 1997), pp. 97-98.
4. *Spurgeon's Encyclopedia of Sermons*, "A Fear to Be Desired, Hosea 3:5," a sermon delivered on Thursday evening, November 7, 1878 at the Metropolitan Tabernacle, Newington. Electronic database. Copyright © 1997 by Biblesoft.
5. John Bunyan, *The Pilgrim's Progress from This World to That Which Is to Come*, (Uhrichsville, OH: Barbour and Company, Inc., 1985), p. 42.
6. *Spurgeon's Encyclopedia of Sermons*, electronic database. Copyright © 1997 by Biblesoft.

Chapter 10—The Opposite of Fear: Love

1. Jay E. Adams, *The Christian Counselor's Manual: The Practice of Nouthetic Counseling* (Grand Rapids: Zondervan, 1973), p. 414.
2. For a deeper discussion about wrestling with doubt, see Os Guiness, *God in the Dark: The Assurance of Faith Beyond a Show of Doubt* (Wheaton, IL: Crossway Books), 1996.
3. See 1 Peter 3:6.
4. *Spurgeon's Encyclopedia of Sermons*, electronic database. Copyright © 1997 by Biblesoft.

Chapter 11—Growing Strong in Grace

1. Jerry Bridges, *The Discipline of Grace: God's Role and Our Role in the Pursuit of Holiness, A Study Guide Based on the Book* (Colorado Springs: NavPress, 1994), p. 7.
2. Ibid., p. 10.
3. "It Is Well with My Soul" by Horatio G. Spafford, 1873.
4. Margaret Wise Brown, with Hurd, Clement, illus., *The Runaway Bunny* (New York: Harper & Row, Publishers, Inc., 1942).
5. Bridges, Jerry, ibid., p. 10.

Chapter 12—God's Strength Displayed in Your Weakness

1. *Barnes' Notes*, electronic database. Copyright © 1997 by Biblesoft.
2. Hebrews 11:6.
3. Such as *Barnes' Notes on the New Testament* (Kregel Publications), *Adam Clarke's Commentary on the Bible* (World Bible Publishing Co.), or *Matthew Henry's Commentary on the Whole Bible* (Hendrickson Publishers, Inc.).
4. John Calvin, *Heart Aflame: Daily Readings from Calvin on the Psalms* (Phillipsburg, NJ: P & R Publishing, 1999), p. 22.
5. Ibid.
6. Of course, baptism also represents the regeneration or spiritual birth of the believer.
7. Sermons (NT Texts)/The Obedience of Faith—Heb. 11:8 from *Spurgeons Encyclopedia of Sermons*, electronic database. Copyright © 1997 by Biblesoft.
8. Ibid.
9. Ibid.